INSIGHT COMPACT GUIDES

Hong Kong

Compact Guide: Hong Kong is the ideal quick-reference guide to this amazing metropolis. It tells you all you need to know about the city's attractions, from the temples of the gods to the temples of high finance, from simple markets to sophisticated superstores, as well as wonderful cuisine and fascinating festivals.

This is just one title in *Apa Publications'* new series of pocket-sized, easy-to-use guidebooks intended for the independent-minded traveller. Based on an award-winning formula pioneered in Germany, *Compact Guides* pride themselves on being up-to-date and authoritative. They are in essence mini travel encyclopedias, designed to be comprehensive yet portable, both readable and reliable.

Star Attractions

An instant reference to some of Hong Kong's most popular tourist attractions to help you on your way.

Central Market p16

Jardine House p23

View from The Peak p32

Stanley Market p36

Clock Tower p38

Nathan Road p39

Ten Thousand Buddhas p46

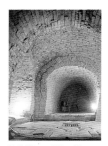
Lei Cheng Uk p48

Shopping streets p41

Po Lin Monastery p56

Cheung Chau harbour p58

HONG KONG

Hong Kong – The Fragrant Harbour

Crossing Hong Kong harbour on the Star Ferry, it seems hard to believe that the city's name is derived from a British approximation to the Cantonese *Heung Kong*, which means 'Fragrant Harbour'. There are a number of suggested explantions for this evocative name. Some people claim that it refers to the incense sticks produced in the villages in the vicinity, whilst others maintain that it is derived from sandalwood. A new theory ascribes the name to the bauhinia, an aromatic flower native to the region, but the popularity of this suggestion may owe something to the fact the bauhinia has been adopted as the new coat of arms of Hong Kong from July 1997, when the territory reverts to Chinese sovereignty.

Hong Kong coat of arms – valid until 1997

The terminology is, in any case, confused, as the name 'Fragrant Harbour' sometimes refers to the entire territory, and sometimes only to the island of Hong Kong, the original colony lying off the Kowloon Peninsula. The latter is also an anglicised version of the Chinese for 'Nine Dragons'. These popular mythological creatures are the benevolent inhabitants of every mountain and are also the symbol of imperialism. A legend tells of the last emperor of the Song Dynasty (960–1279), who arrived on the peninsula far from his capital after being ousted from his throne. When he remarked that he could see eight dragons – the mountains demarcating the erstwhile frontier with the People's Republic of China – a court lackey remarked obsequiously that he must mean nine dragons, since he, the emperor, was also one.

5

Hong Kong and China were always inseparable. When the British flag was planted on the 'barren rock' of Hong Kong Island in 1841, the colony quickly became an important trading post and gateway to China. By the end of the 19th century the tip of the Kowloon Peninsula had also been ceded and the New Territories leased for 99 years to the British. Since that time, the efforts of the local, predominantly Chinese, population combined with the laissez-faire administration of the British – allowing entrepreneurs to flourish here as nowhere else on earth – have resulted in Hong Kong establishing itself as a great international trading post, a powerful centre of manufacturing and one of the world's largest financial centres.

A local of Kowloon

China could have repossessed Hong Kong at any time during its history, but preferred instead to use it as a window on the Western world. Hong Kong's economy flourished as an effective export outlet for Chinese goods, which are now often manufactured under Hong Kong management on the mainland. Without the flow of Hong Kong capital and expertise, Chinese economic reforms would probably not have been able to get under way.

Position and size

Situated between latitude 22°9' and 22°37' North and longitude 113°62' and 114°30' East, Hong Kong lies just inside the Tropic of Cancer on the same latitude as Calcutta and Havana. During the mid-19th century, the British were attracted primarily by the location of Hong Kong island which forms a natural protective shield for the deepwater harbour which to this day remains easily accessible to even the largest freight ships. The total land area of some 425sq miles (1,100sq km) is constantly being increased by land reclamation projects. Hong Kong lies off the northern delta of the Pearl River, through which traders could reach the provincial capital of Canton (present-day Guangzhou), the southern gateway to China. The harbour of Macau at the southern end of the delta, which had been in use as a trading post since the 16th century, eventually proved to be too small and too shallow, and was forced to cede its superiority to Hong Kong. Apart from the flat and sandy peninsula of Kowloon, the territory is steeply mountainous. At 1,817ft (554m), Victoria Peak (*Tai Ping Shan* in Cantonese) dominates Hong Kong island, although Lantau has two considerably higher mountains: Lantau Peak (3,064ft/934m) and Sunset Peak (2,850ft/869m). The highest barrier in the chain of mountains in the New Territories to the north is Tai Mo Shan (3,136ft/956m).

Junks remain a common sight
Tranquillity at Shek O

Climate and vegetation

Apart from the four main areas, Hong Kong Island, Kowloon, the New Territories and the Outlying Islands (including Lantau, Lamma and Cheung Chau), most of the 230 islands that make up Hong Kong are uninhabited. Like the open countryside of the larger islands and the New Territories, they are covered by knee-high evergreen undergrowth with few trees.

Hong Kong and Macau have a subtropical climate, characterised by high temperatures and high humidity. January and February are the coolest months, with frequent mist. Then the temperatures begin to rise and visibility improves. The weather is very agreeable especially during the second half of May, the start of the hot, damp summer. Throughout the year, clothing should be light and made of natural fibres. In business situations, more formal clothes are appropriate, and expensive restaurants often refuse to admit guests dressed too casually. Even during the hottest season your luggage should include a jacket or pullover as interiors are often excessively chilly due to air conditioning.

The visitor who expects to see a concrete jungle of skyscrapers will be surprised at how green the landscape ac-

Formal dress for business

tually is. There are 21 country parks which cover some 40 percent of the surface area, not to mention the smaller, un-inhabited islands. The visitor will have to search hard, however, to find the idyllic rice fields portrayed in old picture books. The population of the New Territories has been increasing steadily for years. Today, it is cheaper to import food from China than for the people to grow their own.

Hong Kong Park

The flora of the region is subtropical, characterised by bamboo groves, palm trees and the odd rubber tree. Even within the city limits the occasional banyan tree has survived. The banyan (or Bo) tree, under which the Buddha achieved enlightenment, is easily recognised by its remarkable root system, often seen above ground, creeping on walls and sometimes piercing through them. Favourite decorative plants include bougainvillaea, hibiscus and orchid. Hong Kong's native flower, the bauhinia, blooms in a variety of colours during autumn and is related to the orchid.

The local fauna is especially rich in insects. Shiny beetles and brightly coloured butterflies can be seen on every walk, whilst the chirping of crickets and grasshoppers seems almost deafening at times. Outside the city limits, mosquitoes make the visitor's life a misery at dusk, whilst many a harmless cockroach may find its way into even the most luxurious hotel bedroom. More surprising are the large birds of prey, including eagles, often seen circling above Central and other districts of Hong Kong Island.

Pelicans in the park

For all this abundance of nature, the development of Hong Kong has taken little account of the natural environment: sewage and industrial waste is pumped directly into the sea, polluting the waters and making bathing potentially hazardous; the air is often thick with the unfiltered fumes of factories, power stations and cars; landscapes and marine fauna are destroyed as mountains are levelled to provide material for coastal infill. The Mai Po marshes, in the extreme northwest of the New Territories, is an important conservation area; as a sanctuary for migrating birds, it is also a favourite destination for bird-watchers. The waters off Mai Po harbour cover Hong Kong's last coral reef, and are home to a colourful array of fish, shrimps and mussels. Lying partly in the no man's land between Hong Kong and the People's Republic, even this hitherto ecologically privileged corner of Hong Kong is now under threat from the rapid urban developments taking place to the north.

Population and language

Archaeological finds on the island of Lantau and at other sites prove that the region had been inhabited, albeit very thinly, for more than 2,000 years. When the British arrived 150 years ago there were a number of little fishing villages

7

Remembering the old days

along the coast and on the larger islands. They were primarily the home of the Tanka, who call themselves 'Water People' because they live on their boats. The literal translation means 'Egg People', which may be due to the fact that they are purported to have paid taxes in eggs. Their origins can be traced to the Malay Peninsula, which they apparently left during the 8th century. Another group of fishermen arrived during the 18th century from the north, from what is now the Chinese province of Fujian. Their Cantonese name is *Hoklo*; they not only settled in present-day Hong Kong, but also migrated further to the island of Hainan and to Southeast Asia.

By the time they were leased to Hong Kong in 1898, the New Territories were more densely and evenly populated. There were no towns as such, but countless villages inhabited by peasants who worked the surrounding fields. Forty percent of the total of some 100,000 settlers were Hakka, whose home lay in the north of China but who had migrated ever further south across the centuries, arriving here during the first half of the 18th century. Women enjoy a privileged position in Hakka society, although they also work very hard physically. They are recognised by their broad-rimmed hats with black veils, and can be seen today working on the remaining fields as well as on the building sites in the city centre.

From the 10th century onwards, before the arrival of the Hakka, a popular migration from other regions of China had gathered momentum. The 'Five Great Clans' – the Tang, the Hau, the Pang, the Liu and the Man – were extended families which settled the area and encouraged increasing numbers of relatives to join them. They made their homes on the best agricultural land available. The Big Five clans now number many thousands, all with the same names. They can trace their family trees back to common ancestors some 20 to 30 generations ago.

The present-day population of some 6.1 million is unevenly spread out. Mongkok in the New Territories has a population density of 14,500 inhabitants per sq mile (5,800/sq km). Following a fire in a shanty housing estate in 1953 which destroyed the homes of some 60,000 people – most of them refugees from Communist China – the government drew up a comprehensive social housing scheme which has resulted to date in more than half of the six million inhabitants living in publicly subsidised housing. Over the years shopping complexes, sports halls, nursery schools, cinemas, transport facilities and other amenities have been added to the infrastructure. From the beginning of the 1980s, vast housing estates were built in the New Territories. Known as New Towns, they are replacing the remaining shanty towns, which are due to be eliminated by 1997.

Encounter on the promenade

More than 97 percent of Hong Kong's citizens are Chinese. Foreigners form a tiny minority in comparison; even during the early colonial days they never made up more than 10 percent of the population. Today, they only comprise 3 to 4 percent. The Filipinos represent the largest foreign contingent; some 110,000 domestic workers from the Philippines have settled in Hong Kong. The Indian minority is conspicuous along the streets, especially the tailors and the Sikh guards in front of the jewellers' shops. The Indian trading families play an important behind-the-scenes role in the local economy. Most of them arrived in Hong Kong during the 19th century from the Bombay region in the wake of British colonial trade. The foreign business community – principally Japanese and American – has increased in direct proportion to Hong Kong's economic prosperity, which shows no signs of abating.

Sikh guards

The official languages in Hong Kong are English and Cantonese. Although English forms part of the curriculum in every school, only a small percentage of the population speaks the language with any degree of fluency. Local residents prefer to turn their attention to the language of their future masters, 'High' Chinese or Mandarin. The latter has much in common with Cantonese, for example the written characters, but this does not mean that speakers of the two languages can understand each other without difficulty.

Night-time characters

In the street one hears virtually nothing but Cantonese, and even taxi drivers and policemen speak little or no English. In restaurants and hotels, however, English is usually spoken, and all official signs and documents are bilingual.

Administration

With the handover of power to the Chinese in 1997, the precise implications for the structure of Hong Kong's hitherto colonial administration are as yet unclear. Hong Kong

Legislative Council building

Loading docks

was never a democracy, but administered by a Governor assisted by two advisory councils: the Executive Council (Exco), the main policy making body of the government, and the Legislative Council (Legco), responsible for framing legislation, enacting laws and controlling government expenditure. Subordinate to these two upper tiers of government are the Urban Council, responsible for the day-to-day affairs of the city centre; and the Regional Council, which looks after the surrounding areas, each served in turn by a number of District Councils.

In the early 1990s, there were attempts to make goverment more democratic by having some members of the Legislative Council elected directly by the people. But regardless of any progress made in this direction pre-1997, the Chinese have the ultimate say and all matters of government policy are likely to reflect developments in China as a whole.

The economy

Hong Kong is considered one of the 'Four Little Tigers' of Asia which demonstrated enormous economic growth and rapid industrialisation in the wake of Japan's industrial expansion after World War II. The island state's beginnings, however, were modest enough. Founded as a trading post, the colony produced virtually no income as it was a free port from the beginning. Leasing and auctioning the small area of land available brought the government less money than it spent on the provision of an infrastructure and defence. The early industries were associated with the port: shipbuilding and repairs, fishing and the supply of provisions for migrants. Trade assumed necessary pride of place, and for a long time the scene was dominated by the two commodities which had actually precipitated the British annexation of Hong Kong: tea and opium (*see Historical Highlights, page 12*).

Following the communist takeover in China in 1949, all those who had cause to fear the new rulers fled the country to Hong Kong. Amongst them were businessmen, especially from Shanghai, which had been China's boom city during the 1920s. They invested the capital they brought with them in Hong Kong and followed Japan's example in accelerating the industrialisation process by means of simple products in the textile and plastics industries. In small factories, workers toiled virtually round the clock under unspeakable conditions for low wages. They created the East Asian economic miracle.

Hong Kong developed into a manufacturing city which, bearing in mind its small local population, was obliged to export 90 percent of its goods. The second act of the 'miracle' saw a larger range of products and a greater attention to quality. Household goods and toys were added, then optical and electronic components and finally jewellery and watches. Today, Hong Kong does not merely copy and assemble products developed elsewhere. The colony has also taken over the development of new products, from computers to the latest fashions.

On the other hand, Hong Kong's dependence on imports has also become manifest. The city could not survive without food, water and energy from the mainland. After Deng Xiaoping's economic reforms in 1978, the interconnection between Hong Kong and its powerful neighbour became an even closer affair, with Hong Kong handling a considerable proportion of Chinese exports through its trading, financial and transport infrastructure. Hong Kong's investment of vast amounts of money, staff and expertise in mainland China was reciprocated by the establishment of Chinese companies in the Territory and the Chinese purchase of shares in Hong Kong enterprises.

Hong Kong thus ascended to the third stage of industrialisation. Work-intensive manufacturing industries were transferred to China's Special Economic Zones, set up in the early 1980s to stimulate rapid economic growth in strategic coastal areas without rocking socialism in the rest of China, and to other regions with low wages on the other side of the border. The city now concentrates on providing services: management, sales, financing. After Tokyo, Hong Kong is the second largest financial centre in Asia. More than 160 banks are represented here and the stock exchange is booming. There seems little reason to doubt that this prosperity will continue.

Hongkong and Shanghai Bank

11

In Hong Kong, support for the pure market economy is still virtually unanimous. The laws governing the social services are reduced to a minimum. Social insurance and sickness insurance have only been part of the scene for the past few years. Tax laws are remarkably straightforward and provide the government with so much money that its reserves are growing steadily. Income and business taxes hover between 15 and 17 percent; capital gains are not taxed at all. Unemployment is virtually unknown, and the 120 pages of jobs vacant advertisements in the Saturday edition of the *South China Morning Post* give an indication of the job carousel.

Watching the world market

An earthly paradise? Definitely not. Long working hours, minimal holidays, poor working conditions, a polluted environment and 10 percent inflation for many years now represent the other side of the coin. The first signs of a crisis are already visible in the land of the 'Big Tiger', Japan. Hong Kong's future path is now largely dependent upon Beijing. As long as China continues its present economic policies, Hong Kong will continue to flourish and will maintain its pre-eminent position as China's economic window on the world.

Historical Highlights

c 4,000BC Archaeological finds on the islands of Lamma and Lantau bear witness to scant settlement of the coastal strip.

c 1,200BC Tools and pots dating from the Bronze Age are also found. Engravings on rock surfaces also date from this era.

7th–9th century AD Apart from fishing, the settlers live by producing salt and quarrying limestone. Probable arrival of Tanka. Chinese fortress constructed in Tuen Mun.

10th–14th century Arrival of the 'Five Great Clans' in what is now the New Territories.

12th–13th century Song emperor flees south in face of Mongol invasions. Two child emperors occupy the throne from Hong Kong, but have no power.

15th–18th century Japanese and Chinese pirates maraud south Chinese coastal waters.

Early 16th century Portuguese traders are the first Europeans to reach the Canton region.

1557 Macau becomes Portuguese.

1607 Dutch and Portuguese naval forces battle off Lantau.

1700 The British establish their first 'factory' or warehouse in Canton.

1773 The East India Company unloads 150 pounds of Bengal opium at Canton

1800 Peking bans the opium drug trade, but smuggling by British traders is rife.

Early 19th century The British East India Company trading monopoly collapses. In particular, the opium trade is taken over by independent British (mostly Scottish) and American traders, for whom the British navy seeks a safe harbour. The British government hopes to open several Chinese ports to overseas trade.

1839 For economic reasons the Chinese imperial court bans the trade in opium once more, commandeering and burning the stocks in Canton. The British retaliate by shooting at Chinese guard posts, sparking off the First Opium War.

1839–41 The First Opium War. A British fleet under Captain Charles Elliot attacks Canton and takes possession of Hong Kong, without permission of the government at home.

1842 China cedes the island of Hong Kong to the British 'in perpetuity' in the Treaty of Nanjing. All Chinese governments have since refused to accept the validity of this and the following treaties as they were forced upon the Chinese and therefore 'inequitable'. Sir Henry Pottinger becomes the first governor.

1856–60 Dissatisfied with the opportunities for trade with China, the British embark on the Second Opium War and force the opening of further ports and the cession of the Kowloon Peninsula in the Convention of Peking.

1898 As a military buffer zone between Hong Kong and the French forces in North Vietnam and South China, the British lease the region between Boundary Street in Kowloon and a range of hills to the north, as well as 235 islands, for a period of 99 years, i.e. until 30 June 1997.

Early 20th century A republican reform movement against the moribund imperial court of the Qing dynasty develops in south China. Sun Yatsen, who had graduated from the Chinese Medical College in Hong Kong in 1892, plays a leading role; he later becomes first President of the Republic. Since the movement is also directed against the opium trade, Hong Kong bans all opium dens. After World War I, which did not affect Hong Kong, the island is dragged into an economic crisis by Britain.

1918 Thousands perish as fire engulfs the racetrack at Happy Valley.

1928 Mao Zedong establishes his first guerrilla base; by 1935 he has taken control of the Chinese Communist Party.

1937–45 Japanese troops attack China via Korea and precipitate a growing tide of refugees in

Hong Kong. Shortly after the bombing of Pearl Harbor in 1941, the Japanese air force destroys British aircraft at Kai Tak airport. The army advances through the New Territories and rapidly forces the defending troops to retreat to Hong Kong island, where they are forced to surrender during Christmas 1941. The Japanese army of occupation sets up concentration camps, deports workers and forces thousands to flee. Hong Kong loses one million inhabitants.

1945 At the Yalta Conference it is decided that Hong Kong should be returned to the victorious Chinese; however, the civil war which raged on the mainland until 1949 prevented this decision from being put into practice. A British military administration builds up the colony again and hands it over to a new British governor.

1950 The United Nations embargo on trade with China and North Korea during the Korean War seriously depresses the entrepôt trade, the lifeline of the colony, and conditions remain depressed for several years..

1950–3 Following the communist victory on mainland China, massive waves of refugees swell the local population. The industrialisation of Hong Kong commences.

Early 1960s Poor pay and working conditions in Hong Kong's factories lead to labour disputes and increasing social discontent.

1966–9 The Cultural Revolution in China spreads to Hong Kong via communist cells: strikes by workers and taxi drivers. Discontent reaches its climax in May 1967 when severe riots break out in Hong Kong and Kowloon following a labour dispute in a plastic-flower factory. Beijing intervenes to prevent the planned general strike, thus ensuring that Hong Kong remains China's secret trade outlet.

1970 The first jumbo jet touches down at Kai Tak Airport.

1972 Richard Nixon visits China.

1975 Queen Elizabeth II becomes the first reigning British monarch to set foot in the colony.

1978 The death of Mao Zedong (1976) is followed by power struggles from which the eco-

nomic reformers emerge victorious. Hong Kong's economic interconnection with China grows apace, especially following the establishment of the Special Economic Zone of Shenzen on the border. China campaigns for the return of the colony.

1979 Hong Kong's Mass Transit Railway (MTR) opens.

1984 Following several years of negotiations, a joint declaration is signed by the British and Chinese governments in Beijing, making provision for the return of the entire Hong Kong territories on 1 July 1997. The capitalist economic and social systems are to be maintained for a further 50 years, but all final decisions lie in the hands of the National People's Congress in Beijing, the parliament of the People's Republic.

1987 The Hong Kong Stock Exchange crashes.

1989 Several weeks of demonstrations against the authorities throughout China. The army ends the occupation of Tian'anmen Square in Beijingduring the night of 3–4 June by sending in the tanks, a decision that causes considerable unease in Hong Kong. Companies move their headquarters and many inhabitants seek to acquire foreign passports.

1992 A politician, Chris Patten, replaces the career diplomats who have previously acted as governors of Hong Kong. Suggested minor changes in electoral procedures are refused by Beijing, which intends to staff the colonial administration with its own supporters.

1993 Sino-British relationship deteriorates to an all time low after Chris Patten proposes an election bill for 1995.

1994 Breakdown of negotiations dealing with political reforms. Discussions about the practical transfer of power continue behind closed doors. At the end of June, Hong Kong's parliament agrees to the Patten plan.

1995 Serious questions remain in the minds of many citizens about the future of Hong Kong, not only concerning the economy but also matters such as freedom of the press, freedom of speech and the right to travel. Deportation of the last remaining Vietnamese 'boat people'.

CHINA

Hongkong

Macau

Antique store on Hollywood Road
Preceding pages:
View from The Peak

Red chillis for sale

Route 1

Hong Kong Island: Western District

Hong Kong is a unique city where, beneath all the skyscrapers and other temples to the burgeoning world of business and commerce, the traditional Chinese way of life still manages to thrive. Down at street level visitors can immerse themselves in the everyday life of the Far East, and there is no better way of doing this than by heading westwards on Hong Kong Island to explore the antique shops, the old temples, the flea market, the chemists, the paper shops, the rice merchants, the pawnbrokers. Wander through the market for dried foodstuffs, and on to the ginseng sorters. Take home a Chinese seal with your name carved on it as a reminder of this 3-hour stroll through traditional Hong Kong, which is best taken during the afternoon when all the shops are open.

The daily trip to the market is an essential part of life for every Chinese housewife. Only the very freshest green vegetables, the fish killed before her eyes and a piece of freshly delivered pork will be allowed to find their way into her wok.

Opposite the headquarters of the Heng Seng Bank, one of the largest banks in the city, is another, recently renovated building, the **Central Market ❶**.

From here, a system of escalators and moving walkways leads up the hill. Designed to relieve traffic congestion in the narrow city streets, they are switched in an uphill direction from 10am every morning, affording glimpses through apartment windows en route and, from the top, a bird's-eye view of the mêlée of cars and people in the alleys down below. A sharp right-hand bend with an old colonial-style building on the left marks the entrance to **Hollywood Road**. The building dates from 1919 and was formerly the police headquarters. The prison, further up the hill, is still in use.

Chinese culture will be of more interest here, however, for the windows of the shops along Hollywood Road are filled with antiques galore. There are tiny snuff containers painted on the inside, every imaginable item of porcelain: dishes, plates, bowls, vases, statues and other decorative figures, furniture of every kind and, of course, temple statues from the tiny God of Literature to bronze Buddhas. Buyers should be aware that not all items on display are genuine, and prices are often exorbitantly high. According to Chinese tradition, even a copy can be a very valuable object, but at present the market is being flooded not only with the booty of grave robbers, but also with cheap imitations from China. Even certificates of authenticity are falsified with great regularity.

Hollywood Road used to be lined with three- and four-storey houses, but these are gradually being demolished to make way for new high-rise blocks. The ★ **Man Mo Temple** ❷ marks the return to old Hong Kong. It was built in around 1842 by the notorious pirate Cheung Po-tsai after he abandoned his old way of life and entered government service. It is dedicated to Man, the God of Literature, who is revered by academics and officials, and Mo, the God of War, who attracts large numbers of policemen, pawnbrokers and antique dealers. The statues of the 10 kings of heaven guard the entrance. On the side wall are litters in which the statues are borne through the streets during the temple festival. Man wears a green garment and carries a calligrapher's brush. Mo wears a red garment and holds an executioner's sword. The altar on the left is dedicated to the black-faced god of justice, Bao Gong; that on the right to the city deity, Shing Wong. The air inside the temple is heavy with incense.

Immediately after the temple on the left, ★ **Ladder Street** ❸ climbs up the hill. It is one of the best-known streets in the city; the name 'street' is actually an exaggeration, but 'ladder' is appropriate enough. Today, the steps are concreted, but it is not hard to imagine two skinny coolies toiling up under the burden of a portly European in a litter in times of yore. Descending a few steps down to the right of the temple, the visitor will arrive in another of Hong Kong's most famous streets, ★★ **Cat Street**, whose name, however, will not be found on any town plan. The official name is Upper Lascar Row, and the nickname harks back to the stolen goods which were formerly sold here. The Chinese equivalent of a flea market is known as a 'mouse market' and the purchasers are the 'cats' who gave the street its nickname. During the afternoon, elderly

Man Mo Temple

Worshipping at the temple

Hollywood Road antiques

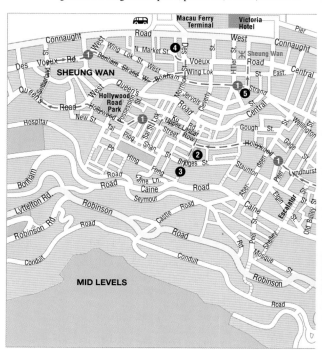

Hollywood Road Park

men spread out mats and rugs on the ground in order to display their wares: amulets, jade, watches and other bric-a-brac. Some traders have proper stalls with a wider range of goods, and the street is also lined with antique and furniture shops.

Back on Hollywood Road, there are still more shops. Beyond a bend in the road, **Possession Street** leads down to the right. It has little to offer by way of sights, apart from a café halfway down on the left-hand side. This marks the spot where a decisive chapter of Hong Kong's history was written. Captain Charles Elliot landed in January 1841 and took possession of the island in the name of the British crown – somewhat over-hastily, as it turned out, because Her Majesty's Government would have preferred an island off the coast of Shanghai. Anyway, more than a year was to pass before the island was finally ceded following a few threatening gestures by the British warships off Nanking, which was the Chinese capital at the time. Elliot was summoned back to England because of his excessive zeal, instead of becoming the first governor. That honour was reserved for Sir Henry Pottinger.

A few yards further on is ★ **Hollywood Road Park**, created a few years ago in the form of a miniature Chinese garden with a goldfish pond, pavilions, arches, rocks and specially planted trees as well as a small bamboo grove – all elements of traditional Chinese garden architecture.

Soon after this the route arrives at **Queen's Road West**, another shopping street where household goods are offered alongside Chinese foodstuffs, especially rice of varying qualities in huge sacks. The visitor will be struck by the paper models of houses, cars, aircraft, furniture, etc. Fake paper money with an astronomically high face value, made out by the Bank of the Underworld, is stacked high in the shops. The items in question are not toys but gifts to be ceremonially burned on the grave of the deceased so that the dead can enjoy the Good Life in the Great Beyond. Come January, the shops are flush with red objects – red calendars, red motto-bearing ribbons, gift boxes and small bags – as the colour is considered lucky. At Chinese New Year, families redecorate their homes and distribute presents. The most popular present is a 'red envelope', naturally filled with money.

Queen's Road West

Turn right into Sutherland Street. At the end of the road and in the wider expanse of Des Voeux Road West, which can be distinguished by the tram lines which pass along it, there are countless shops offering dried foodstuffs, including mushrooms, shellfish and shrimps, as well as fruit, lotus nuts, sunflower seeds, pine kernels, biscuits and

19

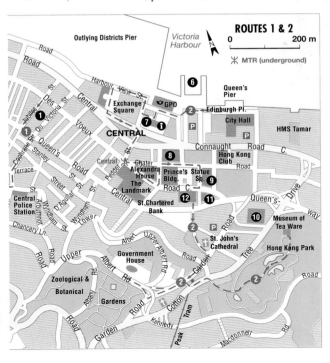

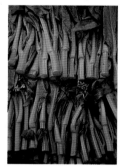

Tea for sale

Chinese greens

sweets. The mushrooms taste especially good; they simply need to be soaked in boiling water for a few minutes to make them tender and tasty once more.

In this district, streets named after the various governors adjoin one another. Sir Samuel Bonham (1848–54) leads off directly from Sir William Des Voeux (1887–91); to be more precise, the street is known as Bonham Strand West. Here are more shops selling dried foods, many alien to Western cuisine but considered by the Chinese to be gourmet delicacies. Bonham Strand West is the headquarters of the firms which import abalone, shark's fins, swallow's nests and ginseng. Ginseng is a root which grows primarily in Korea, in very finely sieved, humus-rich soil and which is dug up after several years. It is claimed that ginseng possesses healing as well as aphrodisiac properties; the latter is also claimed of abalone and shark's fin. Swallow's nests, cemented by the saliva of swallows, are harvested in Thailand and Vietnam by daring young men who retrieve the nests from cliffs when the young birds have hatched. In Bonham Strand West it is also possible to catch a glimpse inside the workshops where these foodstuffs are sorted, cut and packed.

Turning left, the route passes metalworkers' shops before arriving at a multi-storey market building. Many of the people working here previously had stalls in the colonial building of the ★★ **Western Market** ❹. The latter can be reached by following a narrow road on the left-hand side. It is a red brick building with beige decorative brickwork. Built in 1906, it is a fine example of Victorian architecture. Fortunately, when it became too small and unhygienic, it was not torn down as were most other buildings dating from this period, but was restored, converted and reopened in 1991. Today, it houses shops selling fabrics, crafts and souvenirs, with a Chinese restaurant on the second floor. The most attractive facade is on Connaught Road and is best viewed from the pedestrian overpass leading to the Macau Ferry Terminal.

The entire district is full of quaint and practical shops to interest the visitor. To put the seal of approval on this encounter with Chinese everyday life, visit one of the ★ **chop carvers** ❺. These chops, or seals, with engraved characters are thought to have been in use in China for some 3,000 years. They serve as signatures at the end of letters and contracts and also indicate ownership. Thus, pictures were signed not only by the artist on completion, but also by the purchaser. Prosperous Chinese officials would often possess a variety of seals charting their personal progress and development. Scholars laid great store by attractive and valuable seals. In former times, bronze, ivory, jade, amber, horn or crystallised stones were used. Today, the most common materials are clay, porcelain, bamboo, soapstone or plastic, the best material being a reddish stone known as 'Chicken's Blood'.

Chop carver

Narrow Man Wa Lane leads off from a small, triangular square to the left of Bonham Strand. The shops here stand cheek by jowl. After surveying the goods on offer, choose a stone, a script type, and the way in which your name should be written. Latin script is no problem; if Chinese characters are preferred, the carver will have to transcribe your name phonetically by means of appropriate symbols. However, a true Chinese name also has a meaning which is closely linked to the character of its owner. Only a Chinese acquaintance who knows something about you will be able to give you such a name. In this case, ask the person to write it down for the chop carver. The oldest Chinese characters, traditionally used on seals, were introduced during the reign of the first emperor of the unified kingdom (221–206BC), Qin Shi Huangdi. The various strokes are grouped into rectangles with rounded corners to form the so-called official script. Many chop carvers are no longer fluent in this script, and so the newer everyday characters are also used.

21

Depending on how complicated the characters are, the carver may need one to two days to complete the work. However, as the Sheung Wan underground station is just round the corner, collecting the finished chop will present no problems. It is normal to make a down payment. Some carvers can also produce business cards on small hand printing presses.

Shops for browsing

If you are hungry after all that walking, there are plenty of good eating places in this part of town. There are restaurants within the Western Market building, and by its rear entrance, in Connaught Road, more elegant ones in the Victoria Hotel, as well as simpler ones, with tables on the pavement, on almost every street corner in the district.

CHINA

Hongkong

Macau

Route 2

Hong Kong Island: Central *See map pages 18–19*

When the British settled in their new colony, they called the capital Victoria, after their Queen, who nearly rejected the island to which her Foreign Minister, Lord Palmerston, disparagingly referred as that 'barren rock'. Today, the built-up area extends right along the north coast, and its heart is prosaically known as Central District. This is where land prices and rents are highest, which explains why the office blocks soar ever higher towards the sky. The shopping centres and boutiques bear most of the famous names from the international world of fashion. The headquarters of Hong Kong's principal banks mark the architectural highlights of the city. And only a couple of hundred yards beyond the towering skyscrapers you can relax in the green oases of the Botanical Garden or Hong Kong Park. To stroll past the shop windows and architectural sights a visitor should allow 2 to 3 hours.

Star Ferry employee

Harbour bustle

The route begins by the **Star Ferry Pier** ❻ from where the photogenic green and white ferries have been steaming across the harbour since 1898. Directly adjacent lies the **Queen's Pier**, the government's official landing stage where private boats may also moor to take on passengers. The city administration is housed opposite in the **City Hall**, an unadorned building dating from the 1960s. At weekends and during the Arts Festival and Film Festival (*see page 69*), elegantly dressed spectators can be seen disappearing at night into the concert hall or theatre. Information concerning the various cultural events can be obtained from the brochures in the lobby. The attractive inner courtyard is decorated with trees and sculptures, which makes

it a popular place for newly wed couples fresh from the Registry Office to pause for their first photos.

Leaving the City Hall, the slim high-rise on the right is **HMS Tamar**, the former headquarters of the British armed forces. During the summer of 1993, the army moved to Stonecutter's Island as the valuable site was required for other office projects.

The city's last remaining rickshaw drivers assemble on the covered exit path from the Star Ferry. They are delighted to pose for a photo – but strictly in exchange for dollars. Around the corner is the **Main Post Office**. In addition to official publications, the shop on the ground floor also sells detailed maps. The tower just across the road is the 50-storey **Jardine House **, whose 1,748 round windows have inspired the Chinese to nickname it the 'House of a Thousand Orifices'. Jardines is one of the oldest trading houses in the city; its colourful history provided much of the inspiration for James Clavell's famous novels about Hong Kong: *Tai Pan* and *Noble House*. The Hong Kong Tourist Association's (HKTA's) **Information and Gift Centre** in the basement dispenses handy pamphlets and has a good supply of souvenirs.

An elevated pedestrian walkway leads to the waterfront, where one can observe the land reclamation work which will make the harbour a little smaller still. During the next few years all the ferry piers will be moved outwards a few yards, thus creating more space for skyscrapers. This will effectively put an end to the harbour views from the three towers of **Exchange Square** – a bitter disappointment, for an office with a harbour view is a *sine qua non* for the numerous finance companies which wheel and deal here in the vicinity of Hong Kong's Stock Exchange.

Jardine House and Exchange Square

Art galleries frequently use the lobby of One Exchange Square for exhibitions. Between the three towers stands a squat building with shops and an inner courtyard known as The Forum, in which bronze replicas of water buffaloes – which still serve as living tractors for most Asian farmers – can be seen gazing at the fountain and the stylised *Tai-Chi* shadow boxers. The window above the entrance represents a stylised Chinese coin. These coins were round with square holes in the middle, through which they were threaded with string for safe keeping.

The elevated walkway across Connaught Road provides access to some of the most elegant shopping centres in Hong Kong: **Alexandra House**, **The Landmark** and **Prince's Building**. There are boutiques representing all the big names of the fashion scene, whilst the Chinese Arts and Crafts department store offers goods from the People's Republic. The **Mandarin Oriental Hotel ** is a city institution. Cited several times as the best hotel in the

The Landmark

Legislative Council Building

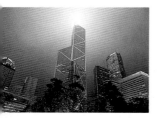
Statue Square

The Bank of China dominates the city skyline

world, it is also a popular rendezvous for local residents who meet business acquaintances or friends for cocktails and sushi in the Captain's Bar.

At lunchtime, however, the dark-suited gentlemen are just as likely to be seen with a sandwich in their hand on **Statue Square** next door. On Sundays, the square and the surrounding streets are chock-a-block with Filipino maids who gather here on their day off. Every November, wreaths are placed in front of the war memorial, known as the **Cenotaph**, in memory of the dead of the two world wars.

The **Hong Kong Club** can be recognised by its narrow windows. The most powerful men in the city meet here. Their decisions have always been more far reaching than those made in the ★ **Legislative Council Building ❾**, the parliament of Hong Kong. The building with the prominent dome previously housed the Supreme Court, the colony's final court of appeal. The foundation stone was laid in 1903, but construction was not completed until 1912. After the court moved to a new high-rise, the building underwent extensive interior alterations. In 1983, as the only colonial building remaining in the city centre, it was placed under a protection order. Sessions are held every Wednesday.

Diagonally behind the Parliament Building soars the new headquarters of the People's Republic ★★ **Bank of China ❿**. Its 1,008-ft (315-m) tower is a landmark on the city skyline. The American-Chinese architect I.M. Pei demonstrated the power of Hong Kong's future rulers with this spectacular skyscraper. In 1982, the bank obtained the site from the Hong Kong government for a friendly 1.1 billion Hong Kong dollars, but then the bank's lucky streak came to an end. Financing problems and construction delays meant that the building could not be dedicated on

8.8.88, the most auspicious day this century. It was not ready for use until May 1990, generally interpreted as a bad omen, especially as the building reaped criticism from the *feng shui* experts for its exterior form and general structure based on multiple triangles.

Dragon on the Old Bank of China

The old **Bank of China Building** , opposite the Parliament Building, seems almost modest in comparison. It is an attractive stone building where, apart from the offices of Chinese firms, the 11th floor houses the ★ **Tsui Museum of Art** (Monday to Friday 10am–6pm, Saturday 10am–2pm), a private collection of Chinese ceramics and bronzes and carvings in wood, ivory and jade. The top floors, where the economic section of the Communist Party once met, today form an elegant rendezvous for their successors, who meet in the China Club amongst choice Shanghai furnishings – not unlike the Hong Kong Club, but facing north.

The imposing building next door is the nerve centre of the venerable ★★★ **Hongkong and Shanghai Banking Corporation** , respectfully known in the city by the understated abbreviation, 'The Bank'. Sir Norman Foster designed the building according to bridge-building principles and intentionally positioned all the technical facilities and services on the exterior, including such items as cables which are normally carefully hidden away. Completed in 1985, the building remains one of Hong Kong's most impressive landmarks. It is worth taking the escalators up to the banking halls in order to appreciate the scale of the light well in the centre.

'The Bank'

The narrow reddish tower on the right is the headquarters of the **Standard Chartered Bank**. From the 21st storey upwards, the floor area is reduced every six floors. In contrast to its major competitor the building's design is based on the octagon, which delighted the geomancers.

Passing beneath the Hongkong Bank, cross Queen's Road and climb the steps leading to the garden of ★ **St John's Cathedral**. The men who built what is thought to be the oldest Anglican church in East Asia (1852) could not decide between the Neo-Gothic and Norman styles and therefore settled on a mixture of the two, albeit using local materials. During the Japanese occupation, the church was turned into a dance hall.

St John's stained-glass window

The path continues uphill. On Upper Albert Road stands **Government House**. The Governor's Residence was built in the middle of the 19th century in the neoclassical style popular at the time. A number of extensions were added at a later date. During World War II the Japanese commandant lived here and added the curious tower. The gardens are opened to the public on one Saturday every spring, but the building itself is not accessible.

Further up the hill lies the ★ **Botanical and Zoological Garden**. The British established botanical gardens in all their colonies to provide facilities for research into the local flora. The botanical garden in Hong Kong was opened in 1871. After World War II, a menagerie was added, especially birds and apes. The 600-odd plant species from tropical and subtropical habitats are clearly labelled. The gardens are a popular destination for family outings, and *tai chi chuan* is practised here by locals early every morning.

★★ **Hong Kong Park**, by contrast, is only a few years old. On the way the route passes the valley station of the **Peak Tram** (*see page 32*). Ornithologists will be amused by the magnificent, brightly coloured birds from the Malaysian rainforest in the 32,300sq-ft (3,000sq-m) aviary. Plant-lovers will head for the greenhouses, but the paths leading past the waterfalls also make an attractive walk. Theatrical performances are occasionally held in the amphitheatre, and there is a 96-ft (30-m) observation tower affording a view of the park and its shadow-boxers who practise their punches there. Children are catered to with a 6-level playground. Finally, a café and restaurant offer lunch and snacks.

The site now taken up by Hong Kong Park was previously known as Victoria Barracks, and **Flagstaff House**, which can be entered from Cotton Tree Drive, was the residence of the commander of the British military forces. This two-storey whitewashed building was completed in 1846 in the neo-Grecian manner and is reputedly Hong Kong's oldest surviving building. Today, it houses the fascinating ★★ **Museum of Tea Ware** (daily except Wednesday and public holidays 10am–5pm), in which tea culture over the centuries is presented by means of equipment and display boards.

Museum of Tea Ware

Hong Kong Park fountain

Route 3

Hong Kong Island: Wanchai to Causeway Bay

Hong Kong's traditional means of public transport, the tram, also makes for an interesting alternative city sightseeing tour. After rattling along between the daily bustle of dark-suited businessmen in Central, housewives in Wanchai and shoppers in Causeway Bay, visitors can do their own shopping, relax in a park or visit a temple.

Introduced in 1904 and still providing transport for 350,000 passengers every day, Hong Kong's trams have remained virtually unchanged since the introduction of the familiar double-decker cars in 1925, apart from the addition of a horn which replaced the original bell in 1993. Redecorated annually according to advertising-agency whim, they run along the north coast of Hong Kong Island daily from 5am until 1am, or even all night on some public holidays. At around HK$1.20 per trip, they offer what must be the cheapest city sightseeing tour in the world.

The main line heads away from Central along Queensway, through Johnston Road to Hennessy Road and then past Victoria Park to King's Road. A branch leads off through Percival Street to Happy Valley to the terminus south of the famous racecourse, making it an ideal starting point for visiting several interesting cemeteries.

One of the famous trams

In Central District the tram bumps past Statue Square and the Parliament Building, the Hongkong Bank and the Bank of China. Next on the left is the many-sided mirrored facade of the **Lippo Centre**, formerly called the Bond Centre, after the now bankrupt Australian financial speculator Alan Bond, but now owned by an Indonesian industrial and banking group. Then come the Admiralty Centre and the United Centre, two mixed-use office and shopping complexes. Opposite is the building housing the city's Supreme Court, followed by a newer multi-functional shopping centre worthy of superlatives: ★★ **Pacific Place ⓭**. The lower levels are filled with more than 860,000sq ft (80,000sq m) of shops, restaurants, Asian fast-food basements, wine bars and pubs as well as a cinema complex with four auditoriums for English-language films. Above lie another 5½ million sq ft (½ million sq m) divided between offices and three hotels.

Pacific Place

Queen's Road East leads off on the right towards the more traditional part of Wanchai. Furniture shops offer rattan sofas, tables and chairs or traditional redwood Chinese dining tables and chairs. The circular **Hopewell Centre** was Wanchai's first office tower. It has a swimming pool on the roof which no one is allowed to use. According to local legend, the *feng shui* experts said that

Academy for Performing Arts

the building looked like a cigarette, and since cigarettes always burn, the pool should be built as a protective measure. No one knows whether the story is true or not. Surprisingly, a few houses further on, the tiny **Wanchai Post Office**, opened in 1915, has remained intact. It served the general public for over 70 years and today serves environmental groups as an exhibition hall.

On the left the tram provides a brief glimpse on the left of the ★ **Hong Kong Academy For Performing Arts**, built on the reclaimed land of Wanchai North. Since 1985, the academy has trained students in drama, music, dance and stage technique. Simon Kwan, the architect, accentuated the unusual ground plan with the frequent use of triangles, even in the open-air theatre. Opposite lies the **Arts Centre** which includes a theatre, a cinema and galleries as well as the offices of cultural institutions. Directly on the waterfront is the vast **Hong Kong Convention and Exhibition Centre**, which includes the Grand Hyatt and New World Harbour View Hotels, as well as Hong Kong's tallest building, **Central Plaza**, which at 1,228ft (374m) is the fifth highest in the world. The whole vast complex is due to be expanded still further by the creation of an artificial island out in the harbour.

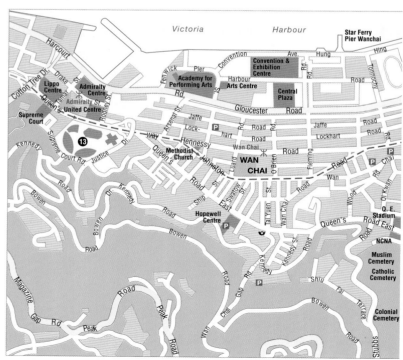

The tram forks right off Hennessy Road into Johnston Road, leading past the soon-to-be-demolished **Methodist Church** and into a part of Wanchai which has retained much of its original character, with its narrow three- to five-storey houses, little shops and colonnades. The side streets reveal a lively mixture of shops, small family businesses and tiny apartments.

The tram rejoins Hennessy Road, the main thoroughfare between Wanchai and Causeway Bay. The typical combination of offices and shops continues along both sides of the street. The trams to **Happy Valley** run along Percival Street, where shops selling electronics and medicines stand cheek by jowl, before turning into Wong Nai Chung Road. There, opposite the racecourse, a number of exclusive furniture shops displaying the latest designs from Europe are located. A long queue of trams marks the terminus. Either stroll through the rather unspectacular Happy Valley district or make your way on foot to the ★ **cemeteries**. Those wishing to continue by tram should simply climb into one of the front vehicles.

The land on which the cemeteries stand was set aside in 1845, when the colonial overlords decided they could not settle here because of the prevalence of malaria. First

Characteristic mail boxes

29

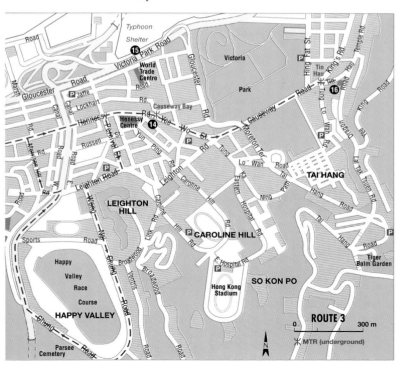

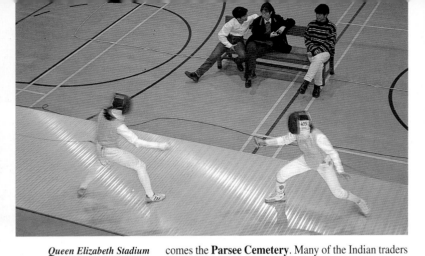

Queen Elizabeth Stadium

The Sikh temple

Jardine's Bazaar

comes the **Parsee Cemetery**. Many of the Indian traders from the Bombay region who helped to build up the commerce here in the early years of the colony were Parsees. The **Colonial Cemetery** is next: the inscriptions on the tombstones tell a tale of illness, accident and military strife. The neighbouring **Catholic Cemetery** recalls the history of the missionaries and is interesting for its Christian and Chinese symbolism. Further still, on a hill, lies the **Muslim Cemetery**. Directly below lies the headquarters of the **New China News Agency** (NCNA, Xinhua), the representative of the Chinese government up to 1997.

A hundred yards along Queen's Road, on the corner of Stubbs Road, which leads up to The Peak, stands a Sikh temple founded during the 19th century. Opposite is the **Queen Elizabeth Stadium**, a sports and concert hall.

Back on Hennessy Road, the route passes the Hennessy Centre housing a Japanese department store that contributes to the shopping mania of Causeway Bay. In two smaller shopping streets, ★ **Jardine's Bazaar** and ★ **Jardine's Crescent** ⓮, cheap clothing and fresh foods can be purchased. The street names honour the memory of William Jardine, a trader who was one of the economic founders of the colony and who, with his partner James Matheson, established one of the most influential trading houses in Hong Kong. Today, the company continues to play an important role in the commercial life of the city.

The firm of Jardine Matheson also owns the legendary ★ **Noonday Gun** ⓯, which is fired every day punctually at the promised hour. It stands by the Typhoon Shelter near the Excelsior Hotel. The safest way to cross the multi-lane carriageway is via the tunnel, accessible from the entrance to the World Trade Centre. The origins of the Noonday Gun are somewhat obscure, although it is known that the opium traders had their own cannon and ammunition stores and were accustomed to greet their *Taipans* – the equivalent of today's senior board members – with a welcoming salvo as their ships entered the harbour. However, the navy considered the privilege should be reserved for its senior officers and ordered Jardine Matheson to use up its remaining ammunition by firing a shot every day at noon. Until 1960, a 6-pounder rang out across the harbour, but people found this too loud, so Jardine halved the calibre by using 3-pounders it bought from the Harbour Police.

The Noonday Gun

Passengers still sitting on the tram will see **Victoria Park** on their left. The queen's monument is halfway along the street boundary. Locals use the park for *tai chi chuan*, for walks and outings with the children. There are also football pitches as well as basketball, tennis and squash courts, a roller skating arena and a swimming pool. During the week before Chinese New Year a flower market is held here, attracting families well into the evening. The same is true of the Lantern Festival, when parents and children picnic on the grass with their elaborate lanterns.

Altar outside a home

31

Just after the park, Tin Hau Temple Road forks off to the right. The ★ **Tin Hau Temple** ⓰ is about hundred yards along. During the 17th century, when this area was still right on the waterfront, the inhabitants of the bay erected a temple in honour of the patron goddess of fishermen and sailors. It is a simple building painted entirely in red, the colour of good fortune. Elderly women from the neighbourhood come to lay their offerings before the statue of Tin Hau on the central altar and to pay respect to their ancestors in the little room on the right. Numerous statuettes of Kwun Yum, the Goddess of Mercy, have been placed in the little room on the left.

To join the shopping bustle of Causeway Bay, take the tram back in the opposite direction for a few stops. The quickest way to reach the other districts of the city is by MTR from Tin Hau station.

For another excursion into a disneyland of Chinese mysticism, take the No 11 bus from Leighton Road to Tai Hang Road, where the ★ **Aw Boon Haw Gardens**, better known as the Tiger Balm Gardens (daily 9.30am–4pm) is found. Aw Boon Haw, a native of Singapore, made a vast fortune through the production of Tiger Balm. A Chinese of the old school, he had the garden of his stately villa adorned with garishly coloured concrete figures and scenes depicting the state of hell in Chinese and Buddhist mythology. Visually speaking, it is an endurance test, but may appeal to children and offers in any case a foretaste of what a life of unbridled pleasure on earth might result in.

The view towards Kowloon

Route 4

Hong Kong Island: The Peak

The world-famous ★★★ **panorama** from The Peak (*see also picture pages 14–15*) should be included in every visitor's itinerary. The journey to the top by the Peak Tram is an experience in itself, and from the summit visitors can gaze down on the jungle of skyscrapers and the harbour, where ferries and vast containers glide by and aircraft circle over Kowloon. At night the whole area becomes a dazzling spectacle of lights. A gentle stroll on the level path surrounding The Peak will take about an hour, after which you should plan enough time for a meal or a snack in these attractive surroundings.

The Peak, at 1,817ft (554m), the highest point on the island, was settled from the 1870s onwards on the advice of the chief medical officer of the colonial administration. The European residents wanted to escape from the densely built-up Western District and initially reserved the slopes facing the harbour for themselves. But transport up the steep slopes proved extremely tiresome, particularly as the Europeans were accustomed to being carried home in litters by coolies – a highly uncomfortable experience for all concerned in view of the uneven paths and steep incline.

And so it was not until the the ★★★ **Peak Tram** was constructed in 1888 that the entire Peak became habitable and the era of the colonial villas on the airy heights was initiated. Until the completion of the Peak road in 1924, the tram remained the only public means of transport on the mountain. The two carriages are linked by a

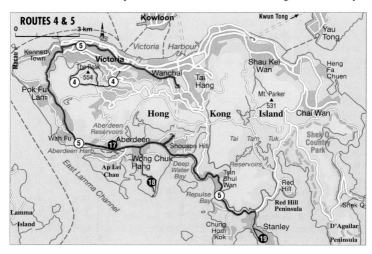

steel cable, so that the downhill tram partly helps to pull the other one in an uphill direction by its own weight. In 1926, the steam engine was replaced by an electric one, and since the renovation to mark the centenary of the tram, larger Swiss-built carriages with electronic controls, accommodating 120 passengers, have been in use.

The new Peak Tram

The green minibus No 1 provides an alternative means of reaching the top. It leaves from the small link road between the Town Hall and HMS Tamar and scales the once inaccessible heights via Magazine Gap Road. The first road link was Stubbs Road, named after the governor of the time. The double-decker bus No 15 from Exchange Square also affords fine views of the city and the elegant villas. The residences of a number of consulates can be distinguished by the fluttering flags outside.

By whatever means the summit is reached, attention should be devoted firstly to the world-famous view of the city and harbour. From the exit of the Peak Tram a narrow path on the left leads to an observation pavilion with a display board marking the most important buildings in the metropolis humming below. Ships jostle for space in the increasingly congested harbour.

Sunset view from The Peak

33

At this altitude there is usually at least a tepid breeze encouraging the visitor to make the circuit of the summit on foot. **Lugard Road** is only a yard wide at its starting point directly in front of The Peak, offering a fresh perspective at every bend. When the city disappears from sight, the islands of Lantau and Lamma appear on the horizon away to the west, whilst to the south the sun is reflected in the glittering South China Sea. The Cantonese name for the mountain, *Tai Ping Shan*, means 'Mountain of Great Peace' – a mood which can be experienced here far above the city.

After some distance, Lugard Road leads into Harlech Road and eventually returns to its starting point. From here, Mount Austin Road climbs steeply up to the real summit, where there is a tropical park with a magnificent view. There is no public transport to the top, but it is possible to take a taxi from the Peak Tower.

In December 1993, the first major shopping centre, known as the **Peak Galleria**, opened its doors. Most visitors, however, are more interested in refreshments after their walk. One possible choice is the **Peak Café**, originally a hut for litters and coolies but today an expensively renovated house furnished with Chinese antiques. Only a handful of tables have views to the south. The alternative is the **Café Deco** in the Peak Galleria, adorned with attractive adaptations of the art deco style which was popular at the beginning of this century, and affording a magnificent view of the city.

Café Deco at Peak Galleria

Route 5

The South of Hong Kong Island *See map page 32*

34

Whilst the north coast of Hong Kong is gradually being straightened out by the succession of land reclamation schemes, the south is characterised by long peninsulas, little bays with beaches, offshore islands and an almost resort-like atmosphere. Of course, there are high-rises here too, but the visitor will also discover numerous other gems. The complete tour of the south will take at least half a day, but one can stop at any point and return to the city.

Buses No 7 and 71 run from Central through the Western District along the coast to Pokfulam and **Aberdeen** ⓱. This route begins in the old centre on Aberdeen Main Road. At the end of the road on the left-hand corner stands

Tin Hau temple

a little ★ **Tin Hau** temple, built in 1851 by fishermen, although today one can hardly see the harbour from here. It is a simple temple with several inner courtyards linked together by round 'moon' gateways.

The road continues downhill to the **Harbour**, formerly an essential stop for every traveller. It used to be possible to glide in a sampan through the rows of junks moored to each other and to get a glimpse of the inhabitants in their living quarters. Nowadays, the fishermen live in the surrounding houses, and the junks have had to make way for the fleet of deep-sea fishing boats. The harbour itself is now nothing more than a narrow channel between Hong Kong and the island of Ap Lei Chau, on which lies **South Horizons**, the largest high-rise residential complex in the southern part of the island. Visitors can, of course, rent a sampan – for around HK$ 50–100, depending upon their bargaining skills – or just stroll along the newly constructed promenade.

Named after the colonial minister of the time, Aberdeen is one of the oldest settlements in Hong Kong. Ap Lei Chau island protects its natural harbour which has been used by fishermen and shipbuilders for at least 200 years. During the early morning hours a wholesale fish market operates directly on the promenade.

Take advantage of the free ferry belonging to the famous ★ **Jumbo Floating Restaurant** in order to visit one of the restaurants out in the harbour. Following a serious fire the restaurants, which offer *dim sum* all morning, do not actually float any more, but rest on concrete pillars. From the window one can look across at the Aberdeen Marina Club, full of moored boats worth a million or so apiece in whatever currency you care to name. The marina opposite the restaurant has another landing stage for the Floating Restaurant's ferry.

Jumbo Floating Restaurant

Lying on a narrow peninsula outside Aberdeen is ★★ **Ocean Park** ⓲, a complex covering 215 acres (87ha) with children's playgrounds, greenhouses, a cable car, shark aquarium, performing dolphins, an observation tower and a roller coaster on the cliffs. From June to October one can swim in **Water World**, a man-made complex of pools, flumes and water slides near the entrance to Ocean Park. From the hilly section of Ocean Park, the largest open-air escalator in the world leads down to an aviary and the ★★ **Middle Kingdom**, in which the famous monuments of China are presented in miniature and craftsmen demonstrate their skills. The entrance to the park is served by bus No 48 from Aberdeen; from Central there is a bus service from the Admiralty bus station.

35

Bus No 73 continues along the coast from Aberdeen. The first port of call is **Deep Water Bay**, an address favoured by Hong Kong residents who can afford to build spacious villas on unobstructed slopes. Opposite the little beach with a few open-air grills lies a 9-hole golf course. In the bay, a flotilla of yachts rides at anchor; they belong to the Royal Hong Kong Yacht Club, which has its clubhouse on Middle Island, just a few yards from the shore.

As the bus rounds the next headland, a housing complex which made local headlines comes into view. In the middle of its gently curving facade is a large rectangular hole into which at least another 10 flats would have fitted. The explanation is simple: according to Chinese mythology, the dragon who lives in every mountain needs an unobstructed view of the sea. In order not to upset him, the builders left him a spyhole. The story may be apocryphal, but it provided excellent publicity. The residential monstrosity was built in 1982 on the former site of the romantic but dilapidated Repulse Bay Hotel. The latter had been a summer resort popular amongst the colonial

Spyhole for a dragon

Repulse Bay beach

Jewellery in Stanley Market

Stanley's Tin Hau Temple

administrators and visiting writers since it was constructed in 1918. It is claimed that Graham Greene sat on the terrace in a wicker chair working on one of his novels. The hotel also achieved a certain fame for its sundowners as well as the tea dances attended by society ladies.

★ **Repulse Bay**, named after a 19th-century British warship involved in hunting local pirates, is the most famous bay in south Hong Kong. The beach has a wide range of amenities from changing rooms and showers to fast-food restaurants, which makes it a favourite weekend excursion for city-dwellers. From the multicoloured temple of the Lifesavers' Association, a large statue of the goddess Kwun Yum watches over swimmers. The No 73 bus continues on to ★★ **Stanley** ⓳. Those wishing to stop in Repulse Bay, however, could also take the No 6, 6A, 63, 65 and 260 buses on to this next destination.

Stanley, named after a British colonial minister, lies at the narrowest point on a long spit of land, the southern section of which is military property. It is therefore advisable to disembark at the end of Stanley Village Road, and join in the lively atmosphere of ★★ **Stanley Market** (daily 10am–9pm). Shoes and textiles are the most common items, although there are also typical Chinese souvenirs. The quality is mostly better than at the Temple Street Night Market, with correspondingly higher prices. Continue through the market towards the exit on Stanley Main Street, which runs past Stanley Bay. There are plenty of restaurants, pubs and cafés to choose from, or one can simply buy a beer and sit on the harbour wall.

The little ★★ **Tin Hau Temple** is also worth visiting, reached by continuing along Stanley Main Street past the bend to the right. The temple lies behind a car park on the right-hand side. Founded in 1767, it is one of the oldest on the island. The present building is unusually shaped for a temple; it is very wide instead of being narrow and deep. Nor are the statues grouped around a main altar, but stand instead on a raised section about 3ft (1m) deep which runs along the walls. Two stories revolve around the temple. Apparently, when the Japanese attacked Hong Kong during World War II, the villagers hiding in the temple saw a bomb which fall onto the square in front. They ascribed the fact that it did not explode to the protective influence of the goddess. The other story relates to the tiger skin displayed in the temple with a cardboard sign that reads: 'This tiger weighed 240 lbs. It was 5ft 10 inches long and 2ft 10 inches high. It was shot by an Indian police officer, Mr Rur Singh, in front of Stanley Police Station in 1942.' No tigers have been seen here since, which may have something to do with the fact that the police station is now a restaurant.

The quickest way back to Central for those who wish to end their exploration here is by bus No 6 or 260, which take the tunnel route. The journey on to Shek O is more complicated as there is no direct public transport link. The No 14 bus runs along Tai Tam Road above the village centre and on to Shau Kei Wan on the north coast of Hong Kong Island where one can then take the No 9 bus to Shek O or change to a minibus. It is also possible to change to the No 9 bus at the roundabout where the Shek O Road branches off from Tai Tam Road. If all this sounds too complicated, the alternative is to take a taxi.

Tai Tam Road follows the coast and affords fine views of the sea. It is not surprising, therefore, to find that the hillside below the road is dotted with houses which are only accessible from above. Then two huge tower blocks appear, one of them named after Hong Kong's rival in skyscraper construction, Manhattan. The residents enjoy splendid views which compensate for the long journey into town. There is an interesting housing estate on the Red Hill Peninsula, with exclusive Spanish-style terraced houses built on different levels.

37

The next landmark is the narrow wall surrounding the Tai Tam Tuk reservoir. In fact there are three interlinked reservoirs in all, surrounded by a network of attractive country footpaths. The road then climbs uphill to reach the roundabout mentioned above, at which point one can change to the No 9 bus. The latter continues down the **D'Aguilar Peninsula**, named after the first commander-in-chief of the British military forces in the new colony. The mountain chain is some 800ft (250m) high. Most of the peninsula is taken up by the ★ **Shek O Country Park**, which is crossed by a number of attractive footpaths. There is usually a fresh breeze up on the top of the mountains as well as magnificent ★ **views** of the sea on both sides. Walkers shouldn't forget suntan lotion, as there are no shade-giving trees.

Shek O is a curious village in which some families have lived for decades in modest huts next to the magnificent villas of wealthy neighbours. The postman's job is particularly difficult as the house numbers appear to be re-allotted at random every year. It is pleasant to stroll through the village streets to its little central square, where there is an attractive temple. During the week, the beach is one of the quietest and most attractive on the island. There is a Thai-Chinese restaurant by the roundabout at the entrance to the village.

Getting back to town is not quite so complicated. The No 9 bus and minibuses run to Shau Kei Wan, from where the MTR provides a rapid return to the centre. If time allows, however, it is also possible to take the tram back to Central.

Shek O beach

Tsim Sha Tsui ferry terminal

CHINA

Hongkong

Macau

A cruise ship approaches

The Clock Tower

Route 6

Kowloon

Nathan Road seems to exert a magical attaction on the shoppers of this world. Every day, thousands of them throng in front of its shop windows before haggling over prices inside. But Tsim Sha Tsui, the tip of Kowloon Peninsula, is also the home of Hong Kong's official cultural programme. Further up the peninsula, life remains more traditional and down-to-earth. Markets selling everything one can possibly imagine dominate the scene until the evening, when the Temple Street Night Market opens. This walk can conveniently be divided into two halves, each taking approximately 2 hours.

Take note of the time by the **Clock Tower** ⓴ – the only remains of a former railway station that once stood here – directly next to the Star Ferry Pier. Don't insist on accuracy though, for the four clocks on the faces of the tower are not synchronised and therefore do not always show the same time. In 1975, the railway station was torn down and replaced by a modern building in Hung Hom but the clock tower was renovated and preserved. Where the tracks used to be, palm trees now frame a succession of interlinked pools. The large bronze sculpture of the *Flying Frenchman* was created by the French artist Cesar Baldacinui.

On the site of the former railway station, the tiled facade of the **Cultural Centre** rises skywards. Officially opened in 1989, it houses two large concert halls and a studio theatre, all frequently used by the Hong Kong Symphony Orchestra and visiting performers. However, it is difficult to understand why the government, despite its determination to create a cultural centre of international standing, ever granted planning permission for the architect José Lei's almost windowless building on a site which enjoys one of the most magnificent views in the world.

Visitors can enjoy the view across to Hong Kong Island, however, by taking a stroll along the **Promenade** – something which should be done at least twice during any stay, once by day and once by night. The tips of the skyscrapers reaching up out of the modernistic jungle on the other side of the harbour soar ever higher, and with a bit of luck, a freighter will sail across the scene, framing the view for photography.

The ★★ **Hong Kong Museum of Arts** ㉑ (Monday to Wednesday and Friday to Saturday 10am–6pm; Sundays and public holidays 1–6pm) stands directly on the waterfront. Exhibited in various galleries are pictures portraying Hong Kong as well as old Chinese works, a valuable collection of Chinese paintings and calligraphy and the classics of the contemporary Hong Kong School. Since the beginning of this century, this group of artists have been searching for a synthesis of East and West, although for many years they were too Chinese for the West and too modern for the Orient. Today, the reputation of their works as 'classics' is denied by no one. Two galleries within the museum are reserved for international exhibitions.

The first museum in the cultural complex was established in 1980 on Salisbury Road. The egg-shaped **Space Museum** ㉒ (Monday and Wednesday to Friday 1–9pm, Saturdays, Sundays and public holidays 10am –9pm; children under 3 years not admitted) is dedicated to the conquest of space and the exploration of the stars. Replicas of spacecraft and astronauts' spacesuits are on display. Next door, in the Space Theatre, the night sky is projected onto the ceiling.

Directly opposite is the start of **Nathan Road**, the 'Magic Mile' for shoppers. During the early years of this century, after the leasing of the New Territories, Governor Matthew Nathan was derided for having a road built through the then almost unpopulated Kowloon Peninsula. The life of the colony took place on Hong Kong Island, it was claimed. In those days, Kowloon was hardly developed at all. Marjorie Bird Angus

39

The modern mosque

Tai Chi in Kowloon Park

Nathan Road at night

remembers: 'Kowloon was a delightfully peaceful place when I arrived. No lorries, a few small buses for 14 passengers, only 12 private cars and a handful of public ones, which you could rent for three dollars an hour. From Salisbury Road to Jordan Road (where the inhabited section of Kowloon came to an end in the mid-1920s), Nathan Road was lined on both sides by large trees. Beyond that it continued to Mongkok through rice fields, not far from the sea. The only buildings were the police station in Mongkok and a row of houses called Oriental Terrace.' What a contrast today – and even more so in the future, when still more high-rises will be built on Kowloon once the airport has been moved.

Stroll past the shops and hotels along Hong Kong's 'Golden Mile'. Some 300yds along on the left-hand side is the modern **Mosque**, the largest in this city and spiritual abode to some 50,000 Muslims. The unadorned house of prayer is seldom open to visitors. Next door to the mosque is the entrance to **Kowloon Park**, which was once the site of an army barracks. Inside the entrance, a few yards on the right, is a path leading to the sculpture garden where artists from Hong Kong and further afield can display their work for long periods of time. Behind is the maze from where there are signposted paths leading to the flamingo pool, children's playgrounds, pavilions and the formal gardens.

The ★ **Museum of History** (Monday to Thursday and Saturday 10am–6pm, Sunday and public holidays 1–6pm) in the centre of the park covers some 4,000 years of Hong Kong's past, from the pots and limestone ovens of Lantau to the colonial achievements of the 19th and early 20th centuries, mostly presented by means of historic photos.

Take the park exit behind the museum and walk down to Canton Road, the site of one of the most famous shopping centres in Hong Kong: the complex formed by **Harbour City**, **Ocean Centre** and **Ocean Terminal**. Fashion and shoe boutiques, sports shops, camera and audio shops stand side by side across several floors. Some visitors spend an entire day here, and Hong Kong must be the only port in the world where cruise-ship passengers can step directly out of the ship and into a shopping centre.

Finishing this first tour in the **Peninsula Hotel** in Salisbury Road will complete the circle. Opened on 11 December 1928, it was the first hotel on Kowloon, strategically positioned near the railway station. The hotel lobby quickly became the favourite rendezvous for high society, and to this day guests sit beneath gilt stucco and potted palms to see and be seen. Since the proprietors added a 30-storey extension, the visual appearance has been spoilt somewhat, but by doing so they have assured the future survival of this legendary hotel in its top location. The strains of light jazz swing through the lobby, and the evening cocktails can be recommended, as well as the afternoon tea.

A break from shopping

41

Rested and refreshed, it is time to plunge into the market bustle. Travel two stops on the MTR from Tsim Sha Tsui on Nathan Road to Mongkok. After taking the Nelson Street exit, continue past the first two intersections as far as Tung Choi Street. This is the scene of the ★ **Ladies' Market ㉓**. A variety of clothing and shoes, household goods, jewellery and watches are displayed on the stalls.

Elderly men prefer the other side of Nathan Road, where the second intersection is devoted to the stalls of the ★★ **Bird Market ㉔**. For centuries, songbirds have been the most popular pets in Chinese households. Their owners take them for walks every day, carrying the cloth covered cages through the streets and only removing the covers when they are hung up on trees in the park. Here, the birds entertain passers-by with a symphony of shrill arias. The narrow alleys of the Bird Market are adorned with intricate cages, porcelain food and water containers, birds, and of course crickets, which the Chinese also keep as domestic musicians.

Going for a song

Continuing to the end of Bird Alley and turning right, the route continues through the neighbouring streets where the shops have been modernised, but where traditional wares are still on sale: temple goods such as statues of deities, candlesticks, incense sticks and sandalwood, and household items for the Chinese kitchen from woks and huge ladles to choppers and chopping boards. **Shanghai Street** is full of shops which specialise in wedding attire. In former times, Chinese brides wore red – the colour of good fortune – unlike brides in the West who wear

Traditional figurine

Fishing for a bargain

Jade Market stall

white, which is the Christian symbol of purity but which symbolises mourning in China. Today, the displays along Shanghai Street are geared to both the Chinese and the Western traditions. Weddings are sumptuous occasions in Hong Kong, for which the entire family sometimes has to save for many years.

At varying times of day, food markets are set up along some of the streets in the neighbourhood, although their existence is threatened by the rapid changes taking place in the area. Look out for the one in Reclamation Street and in the middle section of Canton Road, above Waterloo Road. Modern developments also explain why it is no longer possible to see the fishing boats in the once famous typhoon shelter of Yau Ma Tei. Land-reclamation schemes have moved the coast some 500yds (nearly 500m) further out into sea. Very soon, trains and cars from the new airport north of Lantau will rush past the west coast of Kowloon towards Central District.

Absorb the multifarious impressions of the everyday Chinese world as you wander down Shanghai Street to Public Square Street. Here, take the turn first right and then go left as far as the elevated road above Kansu Street, where a ★★ **Jade Market** ㉕ is held (daily 10.30am –3.30pm). Untreated and polished stones as well as finished items of jewellery are displayed in widely varying qualities. You are more likely to find an attractive souvenir than a valuable heirloom. Jade has a long history as a decorative stone in the Chinese culture. It is usually green, occasionally white, and attracts extremely high prices throughout East Asia. Huge pieces weighing several tons can be seen adorned with delicate carvings of landscapes in temples and palaces. In Hong Kong, the superstitious use jade amulets to ward off evil spirits.

From here continue along Market Street to a little park and a quartet of temples named after the most famous of the four, the ★ **Tin Hau Temple**. According to history, the patron goddess of fishermen and sailors was the daughter of a fisherman who lived in Fujian Province on the coast of mainland China in the 10th century. People began to pray for her assistance after the boat in which she was sailing became the only one to survive a tempest. Kublai Khan, the Mongol emperor who ruled China at the time, nominated her *Tin Hau*, or 'Queen of Heaven', in 1290. In the Taoist pantheon she ranks second only to the Jade Emperor. Her temple stands opposite the park entrance, with her statue against the far wall. Kwun Yum, the Buddhist Goddess of Mercy, and other deities will also be found here. Of interest are the 60 divinities of the annual cycle, the *Tai Sui*, standing in three rows. The 60 divisions of the cycle are formed by the elaboration of the 12 animals of the Chinese horoscope with the five basic elements: earth, water, wood, fire and metal.

To the left of the Tin Hau Temple is a shrine to the city deity, Shing Wong. He ensures justice and law on earth and in the underworld and is thus accompanied by judges and soldiers. Further to the left, in the Fok Tak Temple, are a number of different deities, bearing witness to a strong element of religious tolerance as well as to a certain arbitrariness in the selection of gods. To the right of the Tin Hau Temple, local gods are revered in the Shea Tan Temple, but the visitor will also re-encounter statues of Kwun Yum, Wong Tai Sin, Man, the God of Literature, and Mo, the God of War. Simple stones demonstrate that animist traditions are still very much alive.

Although they spend the entire day in the temple, the local fortune tellers do not really get into top gear until dusk falls. From 6pm they can be seen setting up their tables around the multi-storey car park near the temple. A variety of means is employed to foretell the future: palmistry, reading the lines on a face, or using a bird to pick out a card with the future of the customer written on it.

43

Past the car park is the entrance to **Temple Street 26**, transformed during the evening from 6pm until about 10pm into a lively ★★ **Night Market**. Fabrics, leather goods, fake watches, electronic gadgets, music cassettes and compact discs – mostly cheap-label versions – are the main items on offer. Although everything is remarkably cheap, bartering is an intrinsic part of the shopping experience. The street restaurants of Temple Street or the parallel Woosung Street will provide refreshment.

To reach the MTR, continue along Temple Street as far as Jordan Road. Turn left towards Nathan Road to arrive at the entrance to the Jordan MTR station.

Temple Street Night Market

CHINA

Hongkong

Macau

Route 7

The Eastern New Territories *See backcover map*

Where rice seedlings once sprouted in muddy paddy fields in the New Territories, concrete towers and housing blocks now rise skywards. Visitors can combine their impressions of everyday life in Hong Kong with a visit to a number of interesting temples. The KCR suburban railway provides rapid transportation out of town, so a trip to the Eastern New Territories will take about half a day.

The first stopover should be at Hong Kong's most popular and lively temple. The ★★ **Wong Tai Sin Temple** can be reached easily from Kowloon on the MTR Quarry Bay line. The station bears the name of the temple, and the exit is clearly signposted.

Worshippers at Wong Tai Sin

According to legend, Wong Tai Sin was a shepherd boy in the Chinese province of Zhejiang. At the age of 15, an immortal taught him the art of transforming vermilion into a medicine which could heal all diseases. He spent 40 years in the wilderness with his sheep, before his brother found him. When asked where his sheep were, Wong pointed to a mountain slope where a number of white rocks rose out of the grass. When he called them, the rocks changed into sheep. Henceforth, Wong Tai Sin was regarded as a miracle worker, but as he could also foretell the future he was revered as a demi-god after his death. Hong Kong residents visit his temple not only to beg for healing for themselves or someone else, but also to have their futures prophesied. Within the temple compound is a large chemist's shop and numerous booths for fortune tellers who interpret the arcane texts which the faithful receive inside the temple.

Immigrants brought the first statue of Wong Tai Sin to Hong Kong in 1915 and placed it in a small temple in Wanchai. In 1921, his followers founded a charitable organisation known as Sik Sik Yuen, which moved the temple from crowded Wanchai to the then sparsely inhabited Kowloon. The 1920s building was demolished in 1968 and replaced by a new complex which has been open to the public since 1973. The temple is at its most lively and crowded during the New Year Festival and on the 23rd day of the eighth lunar month, which is the festival of Wong Tai Sin.

Offerings and other items

The courtyard in front of the main temple is on the left behind the imposing entrance door. Most of the worshippers in the courtyard are women, who spend the entire day making sacrifices to Wong Tai Sin or shaking the bamboo spills for the fortune tellers. The picture of the Taoist deity can only be glimpsed at the far end of the ornate hall, which is almost always too crowded to cross. On the right near the main hall stands the considerably smaller temple of the Three Saints. These are Kwun Yum, the Goddess of Mercy, in the middle, Kwan Ti, the God of War on the right, and Lü Dong Bin, one of the eight Taoist Immortals, on the left. In a neighbouring hall, the ancestral tablets of the deceased members of the Sik Sik Yuen are preserved. The next building is dedicated to Confucius and 72 of his most important disciples. The big hall on the far right is used for meetings and celebrations, and the building in front contains offices and a library. On the way back to the entrance you will pass the Yue Heung shrine to the Buddha of Light on the right, and a chemist's shop on the left.

45

Behind the temple and separate from it, lies the temple garden (daily 9am–4pm), which can only be reached through a single entrance. A particular attraction amongst the rocks, shrubs, streams and waterfalls is the Long Walk from the Summer Palace and the Nine Dragons Wall from the Imperial Palace in Beijing, which were copied here on a smaller scale.

In order to reach the New Territories proper by MTR, it is necessary to travel two stations back in the direction of Yau Ma Tei in order to change in Kowloon Tong to the KCR (Kowloon-Canton Railway). The train reaches hilly country after a few minutes and passengers may catch a glimpse of two famous rock formations on the right-hand side. The ★ **Lion Rock** is shaped like a lion's head, but the **Amah (Mother) Rock** owes its name to a legend. A fisherman's wife waited for so long for her husband to return after a storm that she was turned to stone, along with the child strapped to her back. The Chinese are known for their imaginative intepretation of natural forms.

The KCR logo

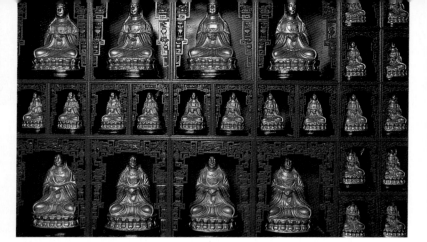

Ten Thousand Buddhas Temple

The Po Fook Ancestry Hall

Praying in the temple

Two stations after Kowloon Tong, the train reaches Shatin, one of the New Towns which have grown up in the New Territories since the 1970s and which continues to expand today. Although half the population already lives in government-sponsored housing, the constant migration to the metropolis means that the demand is as great as ever, and that living conditions continue to be very cramped. The shopping centre and the residential area of Shatin begin on the far side of the station. If time allows, plunge into the masses to see for yourself.

Just by the station and clearly signposted is a footpath leading up the hill to the Ten Thousand Buddhas Temple. On the way is the **Po Fook Ancestry Hall**, opened in 1990. Eventually, some 40,000 urns containing the ashes of deceased persons will be preserved in this Tang Dynasty-style mausoleum. In front of the fence marking the limits of the complex is a narrow footpath leading to the steps which good Buddhists climb to reach the temple, thereby gaining merit for rebirth. The ★★ **Ten Thousand Buddhas Temple** was founded in 1957 by the monk Yuet Kai who died in 1965 at the age of 87. He had previously predicted that his body would not decompose if he were to be buried behind the temple in a crouching position. True enough, when his disciples exhumed the body eight months later, they found it still in good condition. They covered the corpse in gold and placed it in a building on the second level which, however, is closed to visitors.

The main prayer hall lies on the first level. The large Buddha statues on the **main altar**, together with Kwun Yum, a healing goddess and the Ruler of Heaven and Earth, are surrounded by 12,800 smaller Buddha statues, all donated, positioned in the niches around the walls. Very conspicuous are the brightly coloured concrete and plaster figures in the forecourt, which gleam in all the colours of the rainbow. The figures on each side represent the 18 *Luohan*, the most important disciples of the Buddha; in the central pavilion is a Fasting Buddha as well as the animal companions of wise men in Chinese mystic writings. The forecourt provides a fine view over Shatin and the surrounding countryside.

Temple knocker

A branch line of the KCR which operates on racing days leads to the modern ★ **Shatin Racecourse**, worth the detour only if a race is on. Up to 83,000 spectators can follow the races through binoculars or with the aid of the huge video wall. The most important aspect, of course, is the betting, which here is fully computerised.

Race meeting at Shatin

The next KCR station, University, serves the Chinese-language university founded in 1963 as a rival to the English-speaking Hong Kong University on Hong Kong Island. The campus is spread over the hillside and offers few sights of interest apart from the ★★ **Chinese University Art Gallery** (Monday to Saturday 10am–4.30pm, Sunday 12.30–4.30pm, closed on public holidays; a shuttle bus service runs from the station) with its fine collection of paintings and calligraphy from Guangdong Province, 300 bronze seals from the Han-Dynasty period and earlier, and more than 400 jade carvings.

47

Disembark at **Tai Po Market** station and take a taxi to the ★ **Man Mo Temple** in Fu Shin Road. As in the Western District of Hong Kong Island (*see page 17*), the temple is dedicated to the God of Literature, Man, and the God of War, Mo. The inscriptions at the entrance of the temple, founded in 1892, indicate the individual roles of the deities: 'The God of Literature controls the sun and the moon' and 'The God of War controls the mountains and rivers'. On the main altar, Man holds a paintbrush and a sceptre; Mo, who has a red face, holds a sword. Above the doors of the main hall on both sides of the inner courtyard are representations of bats. In China, bats are considered to be symbols of good luck, because the Chinese words for 'Good Luck' and 'Bat' sound very similar.

In the street in front of the temple, a ★ **market** is set up daily, continuing a former village tradition. The people who originally lived here were mostly Tanka, who made a good living as pearl collectors in Tolo Harbour. During the 17th century the village was well known for its market, which served a wide surrounding area. Continuing down the street, you will reach On Fu Road, the site of the ★ **Railway Museum** (daily except Tuesday 9am–4pm). On display are carriages of various vintages, previously used on the Hong Kong–Canton line and originally planned as an extension to the international rail network. The interior of the old station at Tai Po has also been renovated and is on display.

Railway Museum

Sung Dynasty warriors

Route 8

The Western New Territories

Central Hong Kong prides itself on its modernity. Until a few years ago, even early colonial buildings were torn down without a second thought. But a wind of change is blowing through the skyscrapers. In the New Territories, with the assistance of village residents, ambitious restoration schemes are being undertaken to preserve the remains of the old Chinese inheritance in the region: ancestry halls, walled villages and temples. In view of the somewhat complicated transport connections, an entire day should be set aside for the described route.

Lei Cheng Uk

The fact that Hong Kong was settled way back in the days of the Han Dynasty some 2,000 years ago is proved by a grave dating from this period, discovered in the Sham Shui Po district of Kowloon in 1955 during construction work and named ★★ **Lei Cheng Uk** after its location in the village of the families Lei and Cheng. The cross-shaped vault is made of bricks without the use of mortar. Inside the grave, 58 tiny funeral offerings were found, copies of everyday objects which were intended to accompany the deceased beyond the grave. However, neither body nor skeletal remains were found, and experts were unable to decide upon the exact significance of the grave.

Today, visitors can peer into the vault and study the grave offerings, which have been placed on exhibition in the on-site **museum** (Monday to Wednesday, Friday and Saturday 10am–1pm and 2–6pm; Sunday and public holidays 1–6pm). The museum-tomb is located in the middle of a public housing estate at 41 Tonkin Street, four blocks from the Cheung Sha Wan MTR station.

The ★ **Sung Dynasty Village** (Monday to Friday 10am–8.30pm, Saturday, Sunday and public holidays 12.30–5pm) presents a more recent period in a less serious manner. There are replica Sung Dynasty (960–1279) houses, craft demonstrations, and entertaining wedding processions and performances by acrobats, wrestlers and animal trainers several times a day. Visitors who have been to China will find the show a little artificial, and the entrance fee is excessively high. To get there, take a taxi from MTR station Mei Foo.

Sung Dynasty Village

Beside the Song Village lies **Lai Chi Kok Amusement Park** (Monday to Friday 12–9.30pm, Saturday 11am–10.30pm, Sunday and public holidays 10am–9.30pm, entrance fee). There are rides, shooting galleries, a roller skating rink and other attractions, most of which are in a state of disrepair.

The next goal lies directly by the terminus of the MTR line to Tsuen Wan and shows how the coastal residents built their villages during the 18th century and protected them against pirates. **Sam Tung Uk** means literally 'Three-Beam Settlement', a name that refers to the three rows of dwellings placed one behind the other. The homes were all similar in design and were grouped around the ancestral temple in the middle of the walled village of the Chan clan. In the restored ★★ **Museum Village** (daily 9am–4pm except Tuesday and public holidays), a number of rooms have been refurbished with furniture from rural China, forming an interesting contrast with others that display town-style furnishings. Visitors can glean an impression of the architectural principles of the village complex and a hint of everyday life in Hong Kong during times past. From the MTR station at Tsuen Wan follow the tracks back in the direction you came from for about 100 yards (100m) to turn into Kwu Uk Lane. The museum village lies, slightly elevated, on the corner.

49

The next stage in this journey into Hong Kong's past will be by bus, the No. 66M from Tsuen Wan MTR station. It crosses the motorway towards Tuen Mun. To the right of the road the vista is dominated by mountain scenery, while to the left there is a good view of the harbour and the huge bridges built to connect the city with the new airport on Lantau Island. Tuen Mun is one of the oldest settlements in the territory. During the Tang Dynasty era (618–907), a fortress guarded the entrance to the Pearl River. Later, it was expanded to create a naval base. From the 11th century, the Tang clan, which came from the province of Jiangxi, settled in the region and farmed the fertile hinterland. Today, Tuen Mun is another of the huge New Towns, with a population of some 300,000.

When the bus stops at the station, cross Tsuen Wen Road and follow Ching Chung Koon Road as far as the junction with Tsing Lun Road on the left. Here, some 750yds (nearly 700m) from the bus station is the entrance to the ★★ **Ching Chung Koon Temple**. Also known as the Temple of the Green Pine Trees, it was founded by a Taoist association in 1949 in honour of Lu Dong Bin, one of the eight immortals. The temple is principally known for its collection of some 4,000 books on Taoism and Chinese history, and for its more than 1,000 bonsai trees.

Figurine at Ching Chung Koon Temple

Approaching through a huge ceremonial gateway, the visitor first arrives in front of a bell tower and a drum tower. In earlier times both instruments were used to indicate the time. Behind stands the main hall with a gilt statue of the immortal and two of his disciples. According to legend, Lü Dong Bin fell asleep whilst on his way to the capital in order to take the civil service entrance examination. In a dream he saw his future and decided, on waking up 18 years later, to live as a hermit.

Further to the left, ancestral tablets of the dead are preserved in this peaceful temple. A large part of the complex serves as a home for the aged run by the social organisation of the Taoist Association, which also serves visitors a vegetarian meal at midday.

Dragon Gateway, Miu Fat Temple

To get to the ★★ **Miu Fat Temple** either take a taxi or the Light Transit Railway (LTR), a modern tram which runs between Tuen Mun and Yuen Long. The Ching Chung stop is on Tsing Lun Road; from here take No 505 two stops as far as Siu Hong, and then change to No 610, 612 or 614 towards Yuen Long. At the next station, Lam Tei, descend and cross the main road, Castle Peak Road. After a left turn the large temple building appears on the right-hand side. Two powerful dragons guard the entrance to the Buddhist monastery. The hall of the temple is the largest in Southeast Asia; more than 10,000 Buddha statues and paintings representing episodes in the life of the Buddha in Chinese and Thai style adorn the walls.

Returning to the LTR, take another train No 610, 612 or 614 and then disembark at the fifth station, Ping Shan. Walk back a little from the station and then turn right into Ping Ha Road. After approximately 400yds (about 370m) you will reach the Hung Shing Temple, the starting point for the ★★ **Ping Shan Heritage Trail**. The footpath, about ½ mile (1 km) long, is clearly signposted and leads through the village of Ping Shan past several small temples and ancestry halls of the Tang clan to Hong Kong's only remaining pagoda.

The **Hung Shing Temple** is a simple building dating from the end of the 18th century, dedicated to an exceptionally able Tang-dynasty official. He was skilled in astronomy and gave the fishermen weather forecasts, which is why they continued to honour him after his death.

Ping Shan Heritage Trail

Nearby lies the **Kun Ting Study Hall**, built in 1870 by a member of the Tang clan in memory of his father. Designed like a country villa, the building served as a school for the sons of the Tang family; those who came from other villages stayed in **Ching Shu Hin**, the neighbouring house.

Kun Ting Study Hall

On the edge of the village, beside each other, lie three **Tang Family Ancestry Halls**, of which the left-hand one has already been renovated. Ancestral tablets of entire generations or of individual family members are displayed on an altar. Large assembly halls of this kind, which had several inner courtyards, were used not only for the purposes of ancestor worship but also as places for family celebrations and meetings.

Lying in a more remote location, the **Yeung Hau Temple** was built in honour of Hau Wong, a general of the Song Dynasty (960–1279) who protected the two last remaining child emperors of the defeated imperial dynasty after their flight to the south.

Yeung Hau Temple, interior

Beyond an old well lies the walled village of **Sheung Cheung Wai**. Only remnants of the old village still exist, as within the walled compound new houses have been built and old ones converted. Life here, however, seems closer to the reality of life in modern Hong Kong than does the idealised reconstruction in the musuem village of Sam Tung Uk. Outside the fortification, a traditional **Altar to the Earth God** has been restored. It is a small platform, on which a stone represents the earth deity.

Tsui Shing Lau Pagoda

Fields flank the way to the distinctive hexagonal **Tsui Shing Lau Pagoda**, which dates from the 14th or 15th century. It is 42ft (13m) tall with three storeys, each bearing a name related to the stars. Its purpose was to improve the *feng shui*, the geomantic location of the village.

After viewing the pagoda, it is best to head back to the village and to the LTR station Ping Shan. From here travel to the end of the line at Yuen Long and then take bus No 76K towards Sheung Shui. The route runs along Castle Peak Road and through San Tin village; disembark by the primary school which lies on the left-hand side. Turn into the narrow road down the side of the Post Office to the left, and after some 200yds (180m) you will reach ★★ **Tai Fu Tai**, an official's residence standing on the left-hand side of the road.

The house was built in 1865 for Man Cheung-luen, an official whom the emperor honoured with the title *dai fu* (*tai fu* in Cantonese). Freely translated, the name of the house means 'House of the Great Master'. The owner's portrait hangs above the altar opposite the entrance, flanked by pictures of his first wife and eldest son on the right and his second wife and third son on the left. Two plaques record compliments received by Man from the imperial court on passing the civil service entrance examination. In accordance with regulations passed by the Manchurian Qing Dynasty, which ruled China until 1911, the inscriptions are in Manchurian as well as Chinese.

52

The living apartments lead off from a central courtyard, as do the bedrooms on the first floor. The servants lived in a wing off to one side of the main building, where the kitchen previously was on the right-hand side. On the way to the kitchen quarters there is a hollow tree trunk which was used for pressing oil from groundnuts. Apart from the main fireplace in the kitchen there are seven smaller ones. According to legend, Man Cheung-luen had seven sons and thus eventually seven daughters-in-law who all lived with him in the house. As they were unable to agree with each other, they each wanted to have their own fireplace. On the right-hand side is a corridor leading to the rear entrance of the house and to an attractive garden.

The trip back to Hong Kong

San Tin lies fairly close to the Chinese frontier, which means that the trip back to Hong Kong will take some time. There are two possible routes: the No 76K bus back to Yuen Long and the LTR line 614 to the ferry pier in Tuen Mun. From there, a hovercraft runs to the Outlying Districts Pier on Hong Kong Island. (This route could also be taken for the outward journey if you choose to begin the tour at the Ching Chung Koon Temple.) Alternatively, continue further on the No 76K bus all the way to Sheung Shui; change there to the Kowloon-Canton Railway (KCR) as far as Kowloon Tung on the MTR network.

Outlying Islands

Lantau Island

Lantau was once the island of tranquillity. With a surface area of 55sq miles (142sq km), it is twice the size of Hong Kong Island, but only 20,000 people lived there. However, by the time the new airport on the island of Chek Lap Kok to the north is completed, Tung Chung will have become a satellite town with a population of 200,000. But even then, a day trip to the fishing village of Tai O and to the hilly plain dominated by Po Lin Monastery should continue to provide a welcome respite from life in the jungle of the big city.

The ferries from the outlying Districts Pier in Central go to **Mui Wo**, whose English name is Silvermine Bay. The eponymous mine, however, closed long ago. The village itself is unremarkable, so nothing will prevent visitors from immediately boarding the No 1 bus waiting at the bus station in front of the pier. It takes under an hour to reach Tai O at the other end of the island.

Mui Wo street scene

Just out of Silvermine Bay, the road starts to climb the first hills, which are typical of the landscape on this large island. On the way to Pui O, it passes several points where footpaths branch off, all leading towards Sunset Peak, at 2,781ft (869m), the second-highest mountain on Lantau.

Numerous picnic and grill places border the road. **Pui O** is a small village with large numbers of holiday apartments provided by Hong Kong firms for the use of their

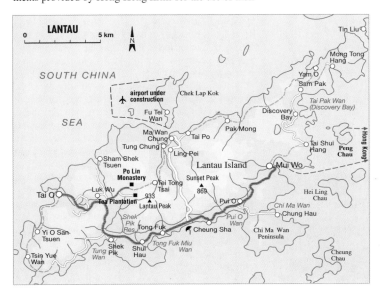

employees at the weekends and during short annual vacations. The little beach is not particularly attractive. From here the road leads off to **Chi Ma Wan Peninsula**, where, in rough countryside, archaeologists have found lime ovens and relics from the Bronze Age which show that the islands and the South China Coast must have been settled from early times. Visitors intending to include an interlude on the beach in their itinerary should go to ★ **Cheung Sha**, which has a 2-mile (3-km) long beach. Even at the weekend it is relatively empty, and the water is fairly clean. A pavilion with changing cabins and showers was recently erected here.

The government takes advantage of the remoteness of Lantau to keep one of the most difficult types of crime under control. On the slope behind Tong Fuk there are several prisons and reform centres for drug addicts, and there is another in Tung Wan, below Shek Pik reservoir. The bus route crosses the 173-ft (54-m) barrage. The drinking water is pumped through a pipeline to Hong Kong Island. From the reservoir visitors will get their first glimpse of the big Buddha statue at Po Lin Monastery.

Beyond the reservoir the bus slows down somewhat as the road climbs steeply, giving passengers plenty of time to study the surrounding mountains. After crossing the pass, the road runs downhill into the fertile Tai O plain. On the slopes are perched several little monasteries with fine views across the lowlands.

Tired cyclist at Tai O

During the last century, what is now the sleepy fishing village of ★★★ **Tai O** was of great importance for the island. Lying on the north coast of Lantau, it overlooks the Pearl River Estuary. Further upriver lies Guangzhou, which as the city of Canton was in those days the most important trading and economic centre in South China. It had its own viceroy and was also the only port at which foreign traders were permitted to disembark. The population of Tai O, by contrast, was primarily employed in fishing and the salt industry, two important and profitable economic spheres at the time. They still play a part in the economy today, although rice farming, duck raising and the manufacture of shrimp paste provide a broader basis, a fact which can be smelt as you cross the village.

Dried fish stall, Tai O

From the end of the car park where the buses stop, turn right into the main street, along which every third shop seems to sell dried or pickled fish. In traditional houses there are no clearly defined boundaries between shop and house; the family may be sitting at the back and eating, or the children perched on a wooden bench in front of the television set. At night, some family members will retire to the first floor to sleep, whilst the others put up their camp beds in the shop. Many of the doors are still

Crossing the channel

adorned with traditional posters of watchmen, or have the guardian figures painted directly onto the doors. In some houses, decorative tiles or ceramic figures can also be seen.

Parallel to the main road a creek separates the main island from the little offshore island of Fu Shan. The channel is traversed by Tai O's only public transport, a flat ★★ **punt** which is pulled backwards and forwards by two elderly women. Visitors must each toss the fare of HK$1 per person into an old box; locals mostly get away with paying less. The punt provides a good view of the large stilted settlement rising out of the mud. For some, these houses represent the best alternative to living on a boat. They also save fertile agricultural land. But the government apparently thinks differently and has slated these traditional houses for demolition.

55

Tai O – a village from the past

A narrow road leads from the ferry to the market place. Here, too, along with the usual vegetables and a few fabrics and items of clothing, dried fish makes up a large percentage of the goods on offer. On the market square lies **Kwan Ti Temple**, dedicated to the god of war and justice. Within the triple-winged building, whose interior is black with smoke, are a number of wooden figures and simple stones before which the faithful offer incense sticks or fruit.

Looking across in the direction of the market place from the ferry, a narrow road leads off on the left towards another temple. It passes ruined houses, the fire brigade, the post office and numerous little huts before reaching a junction. On the right-hand side stands a house with paths delineated entirely with empty bottles. The road on the right leads to the ★ **Hau Wong Temple**, thought to have been founded in 1699. It is dedicated to Yang Liang-je, an uncle of the last two Song dynasty emperors, who as boys sought refuge from the Mongols on Lantau when the latter invaded the empire at the end of the 13th century.

The bottle garden
Hau Wong Temple

Po Lin Monastery gate

Visitors at the incense burner

Buddhist nun

The next destination should be the monastery. Since there is no direct bus link with Tai O, visitors must either take one of the rare taxis which sometimes wait by the bus stop, or take the No 1 bus back in the direction of Mui Wo. After about 10 minutes the Sham Wat Road forks off to the left. Alighting from the No 1 bus and turning into Sham Wat Road, travellers must wait for the arrival of the No 2 bus from Mui Wo to Po Lin. About 15 minutes later, a roundabout marks the end of the journey.

The first monks settled on the high plateau of Ngong Ping at the beginning of this century. When their numbers increased following the founding of the Chinese Republic in 1912, ★★ **Po Lin Monastery** was officially dedicated in 1927. Until the 1970s it was an almost unknown, remote complex, but nowadays the monks and nuns have mastered the art of temple tourism quite well. The building projects within the temple boundaries prove that the amount of money from donations has increased. It used to be possible to stay overnight at the monastery until the government discovered that the enterprising brethren had no licence to conduct such business. All that remains of their hospitality is the vegetarian meal which can be eaten in the refectory following the purchase of computerised place-allocation tickets.

The temple area of the monastery follows the traditional plan and architecture of Chinese Buddhist temples. All the important buildings lie one behind the other on a single axis. Their conspicuous roofs have upturned eaves, and the principal ones stand on high platforms. In the first hall, visitors are greeted by the portly, laughing figure of Milefo. He represents the 10th-century monk Qi Ci, who at his death revealed himself to be an incarnation of Maitreya, the Buddha of the Future. He is surrounded by four heavenly guardians, one for each point of the compass. Behind Milefo stands Weito, the messenger of the gods.

Between the entrance hall and the main temple pavilion is a line of large bronze vessels for incense sticks, and two tablets symbolising the Wheel of Life flank the entrance staircase, which affords an attractive view of the surroundings. In the main pavilion, three gilt Buddha statues adorn the altar: in the middle is Sakyamuni, the historical Buddha, to the left the Buddha of the Past and to the right the Healing Buddha. Prayer flags hang from the roof, and carved wooden frames support the drum and bell, both symbols of time.

The rooms at the rear serve the monks and nuns for private meditation and study. Occasionally, visitors are allowed a glimpse of a very small and extremely valuable Burmese Buddha statue made of white jade.

The newest acquisition of the monastic community is the huge **bronze Buddha** opposite the temple, claimed to be the largest free-standing Buddha statue in the world. Planning began in 1974, but a succession of problems held up production and the official dedication ceremony was not held until 29 December 1993. A staircase of 260 steps leads up to the statue, symbolising the merit Buddhists must earn in this life in preparation for the next. At the top is the Tian Tan, the 'Altar of Heaven', on which the Buddha sits on a bed of lotus. In the Buddhist religion the lotus symbolises purity, for it grows in muddy pools and still brings forth pure white flowers.

View from the bronze Buddha

Inside the altar is a valuable wooden statue of the Bodhisattva Khsitigarbha made of very hard *nanmu* wood. A bronze bell weighing 6 tonnes and engraved with Buddhist inscriptions is rung 108 times every morning, with a computer to control the 'lucky' number of chimes. There are oil paintings depicting the life of the Buddha. It is also believed that relics of the Buddha are preserved here. Bearing in mind that the Buddha was cremated soon after his death and that a number of temples also claim to own relics, a certain amount of scepticism may be called for.

Monastery: interior sculpture

A footpath leads off from the roundabout to the ★ **Tea Plantation**, which was established in 1959 by a Briton. It also includes riding stables and very simple rooms where guests can stay overnight. Continuing past the Youth Hostel the path suddenly reaches the edge of the forest and the mighty Lantau Peak. If there is time you can follow a concrete path downhill. In about 1½ hours you will reach Tung Chung on the north coast of Lantau. From here you can return to Mui Wo by one of the infrequent buses or by taxi. Otherwise, you should catch the No 2 bus at the roundabout to return to the ferry pier in Mui Wo.

57

★ **Tung Chung Fort** (daily except Tuesday and public holidays, 9am–4pm) lies a short distance beyond the point where the path joins the main road. The date of construction is uncertain, but it is known that it was the base from which the Chinese army controlled coastal shipping during the 19th century until 1898, when the British leased Lantau. During this time, the fort served as a police station. It was supposedly also the British who installed the six cannons on the wall; the years engraved on them, however, range from 1805 to 1843 and prove that they must formerly have been in use elsewhere. At the end of the 1930s the local residents used the fort as a school until the Japanese army arrived. Since 1946, the fort has been used for educational purposes again. When it was renovated in 1989 an exhibition room was created with a display of photographs and plaques documenting the history of the complex. Concrete paths across the fields lead back to the village, while the bus back to Mui Wo stops diagonally opposite the fort.

Cheung Chau harbour

Cheung Chau and Lamma

During the week, life on the smaller islands in the shadow of Lantau continues at a gentle pace. Come weekends, however, the ferries disgorge hordes of day trippers who occupy the little weekend guest rooms. It is preferable, therefore, to choose a quiet weekday for your visit. It will take about 2 hours to visit the temple and market village of Cheung Chau or to walk from one ferry port to the other on the island of Lamma. On both islands a visit can be rounded off at a seafood restaurant with views out across the sea.

Both outings commence with a trip on one of the ferries which make the crossing between the islands and the Outlying Districts Pier in Central.

Cheung Chau

The quay at Cheung Chau juts out from the bustling waterfront promenade. Turn left and follow the ★ promenade, which affords a good view of life on the junks and little sampans in the bay. Soon you will reach the first restaurants on **Pak She Praya Road**, where you can make your choice as to where to stop off later on. Turning right either before or after the sports field, you will arrive at ★★ **Pak Tai Temple**.

Pak Tai is the Cantonese name for the Ruler of the North. According to legend, he received from the Jade Emperor, the highest Taoist deity, the command over 12 heavenly legions in order to fight the King of Demons, who had amongst his forces a grey tortoise and a giant snake. Of course, Pak Tai was victorious over the forces of evil. He is usually represented in a sitting position, with his feet resting on a tortoise and a snake.

In 1777, the islanders fetched the local Pak Tai statue from their native village on the mainland, as the plague had broken out on Cheung Chau. Since the island was spared further visitations by the pestilence from this time onwards, a temple was built out of gratitude for the divine intervention. The statue is flanked by the dark figures of Thousand-Li-Eye and Good-Wind-Ear, two popular figures from Chinese mythology who are famous for their remarkable sensory powers.

Pak Tai figures

Each year in May, the ★★★ **Bun Festival** is held in front of the temple. It dates back to the discovery of human bones during construction work, which led the inhabitants to fear that the temple would be haunted by the spirits which had been disturbed. In order to appease them, they put out offerings of steamed buns. Today, the event is celebrated by the erection of three 64-ft (20-m) high bamboo towers, each piled with some 5,000 buns. Religious groups set up stands in which deities and temple paintings are displayed during the festival. The festival lasts three days, during which time the islanders become strict vegetarians. Opera, dance and musical performances take place on the square. Statues from all the wayside and village temples on the island are carried to Pak Tai Temple. On the last day of the festival, they are returned to their homes accompanied by a brightly-coloured procession with floats, banners and dragon dances. The key characters in the procession are always portrayed by children, who wear colourful, traditional costumes. They are carried along on poles borne by the participants, and whether kneeling or standing they remain, like dolls, absolutely still, floating above the heads of the spectators.

The Bun Festival procession

Until recently, the last day of the festival was also marked by the ritual of young men climbing the towers and getting as many buns as possible. He who accumulated the most buns from the highest points on the tower would enjoy the best *joss* during the following year. The inherent dangers of the climb, however, forced the abandonment of the practice, and now the buns are collected in a more orderly manner and distributed amongst the inhabitants.

Photos of the processions of past years hang on the wall in the Brown House. This is a community centre in Pak She Street, along which the itinerary continues. The villagers meet here for a game of mahjong or cards or to read the papers or just chat.

At the next crossroads, the intersection with Kwok Man Road, there is a little ★ **Altar to the Earth Deity** on the left which is always adorned with incense sticks and offerings. In former times, these simple animist shrines on

Altar to the Earth Deity

Surfers in Eastern Bay

which the earth deity is represented only by a stone, could be seen in virtually every district. They bear witness to the variety and differing levels of abstraction of Chinese religious beliefs.

Diagonally opposite is San Hing Street, lined with typical village shops and leading straight into the alleys of the bustling ★★ **market quarter**. At the end of the road, Tung Wan Road leads past more shops and snack bars. A few yards further on stands a huge banyan tree with aerial roots. The incense sticks in front of its trunk indicate that the tree is also regarded as the home of benevolent spirits – but apparently not by everyone. It is to be uprooted to make way for a road extension, a proposal which has been met with fierce opposition from the local inhabitants, particularly as there aren't even any cars on the island.

Continuing along the street, the sound of the sea soon becomes audible again. A concrete path runs above **Tung Wan** (Eastern Bay) and its sandy beach, which extends for over ½ mile (1km). Surfers and sunbathers amuse themselves, and the occasional swimmer dares to take the plunge. At the south end of the beach the modern Warwick Hotel stands sentinel over the bay. During the week it is a possible choice for an overnight stay.

The café on Afternoon Bay

The path leads in front of the hotel and past rocks on which can still be seen geometric patterns dating from the Bronze Age. Archaeologists are still uncertain as to their significance. Passing the helicopter landing pad, you will arrive at Kwun Yam Wan, the **Afternoon Bay**, which is a better place to relax than the Eastern Bay. Above the beach is a **café** serving snacks.

Wandering across the southern part of the island provides a succession of fine views across the South China Sea. There are also a couple of very simple temples, cliffs and a large number of holiday homes and youth centres.

Sai Wan Pier, from where sampans chug back to the village centre, is about 2 miles (3km) away. It is also possible to turn back sooner; the paths are all signposted.

Those planning to round off their visit with a plate of seafood and a chilled beer have a choice between the promenade or the restaurants along Pak She Praya Road. It is also possible to buy fresh seafood at one of the stalls and have it cooked in a restaurant. Evening is a good time to soak up the atmosphere of the promenade, taking the late ferry back to Hong Kong.

Lamma

Yung Shue Wan on Lamma can also be reached by ferry from the Outlying Districts Pier. The bay has a reputation as a hangout favoured by Hong Kong's alternative scene, and you do occasionally hear music dating from the flower power era blaring out of a window, or see long skirts and flowing hair. On some street corners, hand-made batik T-shirts or silver-wire jewellery are offered for sale. On the whole, Westerners and traditional Chinese villagers live together in harmony. Most of the non-Chinese, such as those working in the teaching or publishing professions, live on the island because of the relatively low rents. After strolling through the village, the visitor should follow signposts to **Hung Shing Ye Beach** and **So Kwu Wan village**. The path leads through fields of vegetables and bamboo groves, affording occasional glimpses of the power station constructed a few years ago, whose twin chimneys serve as useful points of orientation. The beach is clean and provides a pleasant interlude, especially as there is also a conveniently located café.

At the far end of the beach the narrow concrete path starts to climb more steeply, and leads, after a few sharp bends, to a hill with an observation pavilion. Crossing the island at its narrowest point, you will soon reach Kwu Wan, Picnic Bay. On the left-hand peninsula an entire hill is being demolished to provide construction material for roads and houses and foundations for land reclamation. Former fishermen now use the bay to raise mussels, prawns and other sea creatures in underwater cages.

Arriving at the edge of the bay, you will discover why Lamma is such a popular destination in the evenings amongst local residents, especially with expatriates. The seafood restaurants along the shoreline mostly bear the name of international hotels in the city centre. There is no connection, of course, but the name adds a certain flair. The procedure is similar to that on Cheung Chau: you occupy a table, choose your fish and tuck in.

Lamma: houses on stilts

Locals chat in the sun

Religion and Superstition

Among the most modern cities in the world, with advanced technology, innovative building design and every modern convenience, Hong Kong is culturally still very much a Chinese city. This is evident not only in the calligraphy of the street and shop signs, the locals practising *tai chi chuan* in the parks, taking their songbirds for walks or playing *mahjong*, but also in the numerous temples and shrines to be found all over the territory.

East Asian beliefs are very different from those in the West. They rest on the twin pillars of Confucianism, which covers all public matters, and Taoism, which provides the individual creed. These two philosophies permeate everyday life despite the fact that they are radically opposed to each other and create a strong sphere of conflict in day-to-day behaviour, in which every individual must seek his or her own personal synthesis. Not only do Confucianism and Taoism furnish the basis for religion; they also explain traditional family celebrations, public festivals and a wide range of symbolic acts.

Unlike Christianity, Confucianism and Taoism have no church, and therefore no institution to govern, regulate and dogmatise faith. Religion is a very private affair with which each individual must come to terms on his or her own. However, the religious aspect is only one small element in the wide-ranging philosophies of the East, and it has very little to do with original thoughts. Instead, it is surrounded by a network of legends and myths, with simple ceremonies and colourful spectacles to guarantee its universal appeal.

Confucius (551–479BC) was the son of a minor nobleman in what is today the province of Shadong. He lived in unruly times, and wanted to become an advisor to a princely court in order to present to the ruler his thoughts on peace and order. In doing so he referred to the 'ideal rulers' Yao and Shun, whose only disadvantage was that their origins lay in the world of mythology. The state declared the theories of Confucius to be largely idealistic. Confucius saw the 'ideal' society as consisting of a strict hierarchy in which rulers had the power to make decisions for ministers, fathers for sons, husbands for wives and older brothers for younger ones. Only relationships between friends were regarded as equal. In return, the rulers were required to treat their subjects with benevolence and to care for them. The 'school' of Confucius had virtually no influence during his lifetime and the Master was denied a high position and had to eke out an existence as a wandering tutor. His pupils, however, achieved considerable influence and, in their position as princely advisors,

Mahjong in progress

63

Religion is a private affair

developed the theory of the 'mandate of Heaven', which was to legitimise the ruler's claim to power. During the Han Dynasty (206BC–220AD), the emperor was so convinced by the doctrines of Confucius that he added paragraphs concerning the maintenance of power and declared them to be the national doctrine. The effects can be observed in some East Asian countries to this day where societies are characterised by lack of social mobility and authoritarian regimes govern the political scene.

Strong family ties emanate from the respect due to one's ancestors, a duty instilled into the eldest son. It is believed that the soul leaves the body at death but finds no rest for three generations, haunting and influencing the lives of those left behind. In order to ensure that the soul is contented it must be given those things which it needed during its earthly life. On special days set aside for paying tribute to one's ancestors, fake paper money is burned on the grave or in the temple, borne by smoke into the spirit world. The souls thus acquire god-like status: both are revered but not worshipped. Neither the souls of the departed nor the gods are seen as capable of human action, and the tablets devoted to ancestors or figures of divinities are seen as memorials or means of concentration.

Ancestry Hall

This belief provides the link to Taoism, which concentrates exclusively on the individual and his ability to find his individual *Tao*, in other words an attitude which is at one with his nature. The Taoist often finds this in the behaviour pattern known as the *wu wei*, which is frequently translated as 'way'. This is a form of non-interference which should not be seen as passivity but which involves activity in harmony with nature.

Yin and yang symbols

The development of Taoism is ascribed to the hermit Lao Tzu (c 6th century BC), although there is evidence that the *Tao-te Ching* ('The Way and the Virtue') is a later collection of aphorisms. Closely linked to Taoism is the idea of *yin* and *yang*, two opposing forces which each bear the essence of the other within them and which find balance in a perfect synthesis. The *yang* stands for masculinity, strength, hardness, brightness, heat, activity and the south; the *yin* is the symbol of femininity, weakness, softness, darkness, cold, passivity and the north.

The influence of Taoism in art cannot be overestimated. Painters, calligraphers and poets were limited by clearly laid-down traditions regarding technique and subject, but in the execution of their art and their attitude to life they devoted themselves to Taoism. The scenes depicted in the typical landscape paintings on rice paper were copied time and time again and reveal Taoist thoughts. Vast precipitous mountains swathed in clouds dominate the picture in which human figures are insignificant. Nature is seen as the all-powerful element in which man should seek his place without contradiction as far as this is possible.

Taoism, like Confucianism, was originally not a religion. It developed its popular forms only after the arrival of Buddhism in China, i.e. in about 65AD. Mahayana Buddhism, or the Way of the Greater Vehicle, spread throughout China. This doctrine proclaims that deliverance and entry into nirvana as a release from all earthly suffering can also be achieved with the assistance of the *bodhisattvas*. These are Buddhist saints who postpone their own enlightenment in order to help others. The best-known *bodhisattva* is Avalokiteshhvara, who underwent a gender transformation in China to become Guan Yin (Kwun Yun in Cantonese), the much-loved Goddess of Mercy.

Taoism also acquired a vast pantheon of gods. Pride of place is occupied by the Jade Emperor, followed by divinities of lesser importance. The second level is occupied by the Eight Immortals, originally historic personages of the 7th–10th century about whom legends later grew, relating the ways in which they achieved their immortality. The Eight Immortals live on the Island of the Blessed and can return to earth to help mankind in a similar manner to the *bodhisattvas*. The seven men and one woman each possess a characteristic sign by which they can be recognised and which will frequently be spotted in stylised form adorning the poles in the temples of Hong Kong: a fly-swatter, a gourd, a basket of flowers, etc. The third level is occupied by earthly beings who are revered as if they were gods. Most of these are historic personages such as poets, doctors, officials and generals who distinguished themselves in some way and who later acquired legendary status. There are vast numbers of them, most only being known on a local or regional level. Hong Kong's best-loved Taoist divinity is Tin Hau, the patroness of fishermen and sailors. She occupies the highest level as the Queen of Heaven.

The Taoist philosophy of nature also gave rise to the geomancy known in Hong Kong as *feng shui*, literally translated as 'wind-water'. *Feng shui* asserts that buildings should also harmonise with their surroundings, that they should be protected and should have no sharp corners. The most favourable location for a building is with a mountain behind, if possible to the north. The south and the front side of the building should open onto a plain. The explanation is simple and practical: the ideas arose in north China, where icy winds and sandstorms from the Mongolian plains blow down from the north, and where having a protective mountain makes sense. A mountain to the south, on the other hand, would block out the sun which is as essential for life as water. Apart from influencing the site of residential buildings, the principles of *feng shui* are used to position the graves of ancestors. Since the in-

65

Buddhist painting, Min Fat

Stone lions divert bad currents

fluence of ancestors on the living is so crucial, it is essential that they should be laid to rest in the most favourable location.

This original idea has given way to countless stories and myths, including that of a dragon which supposedly lives in every mountain. This is an area where the Chinese are masters of pragmatism – especially those who live in Hong Kong, where the most favourable locations for buildings are often compromised by the shortage of land. Minor constructional additions, like a strategically placed fountain or a stone lion, can divert bad currents; mirrors can drive away evil spirits. The *feng shui* experts are masters at finding ways and means of justifying an exception to the rule. It should not be assumed, however, that everyone in Hong Kong believes implicitly in all these stories. They are symbols which remind the community of its roots and encourage communication in an utterly practical manner. Some manifestations – like the hole in the wall of the building in Repulse Bay – are simply publicity stunts, and very good ones at that, for every tourist is familiar with the story.

The significance of numbers also makes an interesting game. In many societies, the number 8 is a lucky number, because it can be repeated an infinite number of times without removing the pen from the paper. In China, too, the number 8 symbolises infinity and eternal life. It is thus not a coincidence that the Tao immortals are eight in number. In Hong Kong, moreover, the Cantonese names for several numbers sound similar to words with completely different meanings. Thus, the word for 'one' is associated with the word for 'must', 'two' is linked to 'easy' or 'light' and the word for 'eight' to 'excess'. Only the number 4 is a bad omen, for the Cantonese word for it sounds like that for 'death'. People have made up an infinite variety of ways to support this superstition; for example, Hong Kong citizens may make sure that their car registration plates consist only of 'good' numbers. Number 28 could be taken to mean 'win excess easily' or, better still, a quadrupling of the number of excess: '8888'. Most prestigious of all are the one-digit numbers. The government shrewdly auctions such numbers and uses the income to finance social projects.

Number combinations containing the number '4', on the other hand, are avoided. Worst of all is '14', for it means 'must die'. For this reason, many buildings have no 14th floor as no one would want to live on this level. Sometimes, the number '13' is also missing in order to appease Western superstitions. The most auspicious day of this century was, of course, 8.8.88, a day on which the registry offices had to put in overtime performing marriage ceremonies, and countless new businesses were founded.

Festivals and Folklore

Dazzling effigies

Traditional festivals are a natural product of religious and superstitious beliefs and mostly honour individual gods or ancestors. They follow the ancient Chinese lunar calendar and the cycle begins with the New Year's festival on the first full moon between mid-January and mid-February. Families spring-clean their homes, buy new furnishings or possessions, redecorate – especially with 'lucky' pictures of fish, because, like certain numbers, the words 'luck' and 'fish' are near homonyms. Above all, the ancestral altar must be cleaned, as according to legend, the Kitchen God ascends to heaven on the eve of the New Year to give the Jade Emperor a report on the family. In order to ensure that he tells only the sweetest stories, some Chinese smear the mouth of his image with honey.

67

According to Confucian tradition, superiors must show their subordinates their goodwill at **New Year**. Nowadays, this usually involves gifts of money in little red envelopes, red being the colour of good fortune. Children and domestics as well as everyone else in a subservient position will be remembered on this occasion. People wish each other *kung hei fat choi*, or much prosperity and success in the New Year. The festival itself, however, is spent at home feasting and celebrating with the family. Many take the opportunity to visit relatives across the border, and the city grinds to a halt for several days. Previously, vast firework displays would chase away the evil spirits. Today, however, the law is victorious over tradition, and private firework displays are banned on safety grounds. By way of compensation, the government sends a few millions' worth of fireworks rocketing into the air above the harbour every year.

Chinese New Year – a time for giving and celebrating

Officially, the end of New Year festivities is marked on the 15th day with a **Lantern Festival** (*Yuen Siu*), but

Dragon Boat Festival

this is seldom celebrated these days. Much more important is the **Festival of the Dead** (*Qing Ming*), which occurs on 4 April. Thousands of people visit the cemeteries to pay respect to the dead by cleaning the graves, lighting incense and offering gifts.

Although **Tin Hau's** birthday on the 23rd day of the third lunar month is not an official holiday, it is marked by numerous processions in which the statues of the goddess are carried through the streets or, more appropriately, loaded into boats for a ceremonial patrol of the bays dotting the coastline. There are dragon dances, local opera performances and many other spectacles.

The religious origins of the **Dragon Boat Festival** are obscure today, although ceremonies to dedicate the boats still mark the start of the proceedings. The background, however, could not be more to the point. It is said that during the Zhou Dynasty (officially 1122–221BC), the loyal official Qu Yuan suggested a number of reforms, which were, however, all turned down by the corrupt ruling prince. In despair, Qu Yuan decided to commit suicide and threw himself into the river. Too late to save him, a group of fishermen threw rice dumplings into the water to prevent the fishes from eating his body. To this day, the incident is marked by eating glutinous rice cakes filled with meat called *zhongzi*, and holding boat races. During the entire month of June, teams train in the bays for the qualifying contest. The **International Dragon Boat Races** have become an important event in the sporting calendar and each year, teams from some 15 countries participate. Sitting in pairs, and to the beat of a large drum, the open, wooden boats are paddled by a crew of between 20 and 50, depending on the size of the boat. The races take the form of a competition held one weekend in June off Tsim Sha Tsui East; there are even rumours that the sport is to be included at the Olympic Games.

The mid-Autumn Festival, also known as the **Moon Festival**, is held during the September full moon. It is a sort of harvest festival, during which sweet delicacies called mooncakes, with a bean paste and egg filling, are eaten. The second **Festival of the Dead**, *Chueng Yeung*, takes place a few weeks later, in October. Once again, the graves are cleaned and offerings are made.

As far as Chinese theatre and music are concerned, there are occasional performances of Chinese opera, although these mostly occur as part of the temple festivals. Traditional Chinese music is actively encouraged by the administration to ensure that it reaches the general public. Most art exhibitions are arranged with a view to selling the works on display – a fact which underlines Hong Kong's commercial attitude.

68

Western Culture

The metropolis has plenty to offer in the field of contemporary high-rise architecture. Norman Foster used bridge-building techniques in his Hong Kong and Shanghai Bank, whilst I.M. Pei chose a series of triangular surfaces for his famous landmark, the Bank of China. In a renaissance of more playful forms some buildings have tent-like roofs in imitation copper, whilst many others depart from the traditional rectangular ground plan.

The Lippo Centre

Architecture is the most visible manifestation of Western culture in Hong Kong. A search for the performing arts is rather more difficult. The government is devoting much energy to the organisation of festivals in an attempt to disprove the city's reputation as a purely commercial centre. Despite wide public interest, however, these events often seem artificial, as if those attending are not at home in this culture.

The **Fringe Festival** (January/February), arranged by private groups and acting as a curtain raiser to the **Hong Kong Arts Festival** (February/March), kicks off the annual programme. The Fringe traditionally offered more avant-garde and experimental art while the Arts Festival wooed audiences with a mainstream programme of performances by orchestras and soloists, and theatre and ballet companies from all over the world, with an increasing emphasis on Asian theatre. In recent years, however, the Fringe Festival has established a firm identity of its own, and increasingly it seems as if the two festivals are competing to offer similar programmes.

Academy for Performing Arts

It will come as no surprise to learn that Hong Kong, as a centre of the film-making industry, should also have its own **Film Festival** (April). More than 100 films from all over the world are presented over a period of two weeks. These are likely to include two or three premieres, usually of Chinese films. Retrospectives, special themes and exhibitions complete the festival.

Modern art is a more complicated affair. Since the 1950s, Hong Kong artists have used the conflict between Eastern and Western culture creatively to discover new ways of presenting their ideas. Initially scorned by Hong Kong society, their works are now displayed in the Hong Kong Museum of Arts as well as in public buildings such as the Cultural Centre.

There are hundreds of art galleries in Hong Kong. Many of them close almost as quickly as they open, but the local papers provide listings of current exhibitions. The works on display are mostly also for sale. The **Art Fair** (November) also offers famous names from the West, as the wealthiest purchasers are more likely to be found in Asia these days.

Food and Drink

Opposite: Some local delicacies

The ethnic melting pot of Hong Kong has created a gourmet's paradise, which offers what is generally accepted to be the best Chinese food in the world. Apart from the various Chinese cuisines described below, cuisines from neighbouring Asian countries – Thai, Japanese, Korean, Indian and Vietnamese – are also found in abundance in Hong Kong and are of excellent quality. Western cuisine is well represented, too, albeit mostly in restaurants of the more expensive hotels.

Dim sum

Dim sum

One of Hong Kong's traditional delicacies is *dim sum*, little snacks originally served with tea at breakfast time, but which today is more popular as a light lunch. Most *dim sum* are small savoury appetisers made of dough, filled with vegetables, meat or seafood, and steamed in bamboo baskets over boiling water. However, *dim sum* can also include deep-fried spring rolls, sweet cakes and the more exotic braised chicken's feet. In traditional *dim sum* restaurants, elderly waitresses push around trolleys from which guests can help themselves to whatever dishes take their fancy. Each plate taken is marked on a card at the table and added to the final bill. In some restaurants today, *dim sum* menus have replaced the trolleys, making the task of deciding what to eat more difficult.

Cantonese cuisine

Your favourite Chinese restaurant back home is most likely to serve Cantonese cuisine as the region around Guangzhou is where many Chinese emigrants originated. Many Chinese restaurants in Europe and the US have adapted their food to appeal to the residents of their adopted homeland, but generally, native Cantonese cuisine does not overpower the senses with the use of pungent sauces or spices. As in any coastal province, fish

Fish is a major part of the diet

and other seafood are popular ingredients, usually steamed or braised very quickly and served with a simple soy-based sauce. Chicken and pork are the most popular types of meat used in Cantonese dishes. An innumerable variety of green leafy vegetables are eaten, usually briefly stir-fried in a wok with oyster sauce. In a typical Cantonese meal, steamed white rice is always the staple, accompanied by an array of side dishes, usually a soup, a meat or seafood dish and a vegetable stir fry.

Speciality dishes, using ingredients which are rare and believed to have fortifying effects, are usually reserved for grand wedding celebrations and other festive occasions. Shark's fin, said to be an aphrodisiac, is prepared as soup; abalone, a type of shellfish, is also claimed to have a strengthening effect; bird's nests, purported to ease asthmatic attacks, utilises the saliva which swallows produce to bind their nests together on high, rocky cliffs. All these specialities are extremely expensive.

Dried produce

Other Chinese cuisines

In the cuisine of Northern China, noodles and steamed rolls accompany most meals rather than rice because wheat is a major crop on the vast northern plains. Filled dumplings (*jiaozi*) are a popular speciality. Another well-loved dish in Hong Kong is Peking Duck. The name refers to the special manner of preparation: the skin of the bird is inflated like a balloon and basted with a special marinade before it is roasted in a very hot oven. When cooked, the crispy skin, but not the meat, is sliced into bite-sized pieces and served with a thin pancake, fresh scallions and *hoisin* sauce. The duck meat is used to cook other dishes accompanying the meal.

Advance orders must be placed for Beggar's Chicken, which is stuffed with cabbage and spices and wrapped in lotus leaves before it is encased in clay and baked for several hours. The waiter smashes the clay casing at the guest's table, making a great show of it and releasing the aromas of the now very tender bird.

The Mongolian grill also originated in the north. Choose your ingredients from a buffet and either give them to the chef to cook or prepare them yourself on a hotplate at the table. Or you can opt for the fondue-like Mongolian fire pot, in which raw meats, seafood, tofu, chopped vegetables and an array of other ingredients are cooked in boiling stock. The food is retrieved using chopsticks or little wire baskets.

The southwestern province of Szechuan is famous for its spicy cuisine, which usually features garlic, fennel, coriander and copious quantities of chilli peppers. Cooking methods include steaming, simmering and marinating. In Hong Kong, prawns prepared Szechuan-style are absolutely delicious; the popular smoked duck is made with ginger, cinnamon, peppercorns and orange peel.

Culinary specialities from the province of Hunan, like those of Szechuan, tend to be spicy. Hunan dishes include consommé with mashed pigeon, duck tongues served with mustard sauce, and fish coated with preserved fish paste.

Another highly individual Chinese cuisine is that from the region around Shanghai. It is generally more starchy and 'warming' than Cantonese food. The main ingredients used include salt- and freshwater fish, eels, prawns and crabs. Some dishes are flavoured with citrus fruits, especially orange and lemon. The ubiquitous sweet-and-sour fried fish originated in this region.

72

Preparing prawns
A soup vendor

Drinks

The perfect compliment to Chinese food is Chinese tea, served plain in little cups. It is claimed that tea has purgative and digestive properties, which is why a small dish is always drunk before and after the meal. In most restaurants, the tea is placed automatically on every table. It is also reputedly a good solvent for fat, an important quality in view of the oily texture of some Chinese dishes. Beer is another popular accompaniment and is better than Chinese wine, which is very sweet. European wines are extremely expensive in Hong Kong and usually not even offered at Chinese restaurants. Somewhat less costly are wines from California and Australia. A fiery Chinese schnapps makes a good digestif; Maotai is the best-known example, a potent brew made of sorghum.

An alternative to tea

Food culture and etiquette

In Asia, eating is always a group activity. People enjoy going to a Chinese restaurant with a large group of friends because this provides the opportunity for boisterous conversations and the chance to order a large variety of contrasting dishes. Either the host chooses for his guests or a consensus is arrived at with a colourful parade of meat, fish and vegetable dishes, in which sweet, sour, hot, salty and bitter flavours contrast in much the same way as textures: crisp and soft, juicy and dry. All serving dishes are placed in the middle of the table and the guests simply help themselves using chopsticks. At formal banquets it is considered polite to place the choicest morsels on the guest's plate with the aid of chopsticks or a serving spoon. This procedure is repeated during each course, and toasts are exchanged several times.

If tea is being drunk, the host always tops up the cups of his guests before serving himself. The guest should

73

Tucking in at the Night Market

indicate his thanks by rapping lightly several times on the table with the knuckles of his right hand. This custom is based on an old story where one of the Chinese emperors, who liked to travel incognito throughout his realm, arrived at an inn accompanied by his official entourage. He courteously poured tea into the dishes of his subjects, who normally would have showed their gratitude by kowtowing to him. By doing so, however, they would have betrayed the emperor's identity. To avoid this, one of the courtiers suggested bending two fingers and rapping on the table in imitation of the kowtow, but without being noticed by onlookers.

When the teapot is empty, the lid is removed and replaced so that it only half covers the pot. The waiter or waitress will then pour fresh water onto the tea leaves. There is a story behind this practice, too. An elderly Chinese liked to spend much of his time chatting with his friends or reading in a tea house. One day, he had his pet songbird with him, and not knowing where to put it, he hid the bird in the empty teapot. A waiter came to refill the pot, but when he lifted the lid, the valuable songbird escaped. The old man sued the owner of the tea house for compensation; the latter then issued the instruction that all guests remove the lids of their teapots themselves.

By the time the plates are cleaned of the last morsel – although it is polite to leave a little to indicate the abundance of the meal – the company usually breaks up fairly quickly. It is not customary to remain seated in order to chat once the meal is over. The bill is usually settled by a single person. It would cause considerable uproar and embarrassment in any Hong Kong restaurant, irrespective of type, if one were to request separate bills. It is better to repay an invitation in kind.

Street poultry seller

Restaurant selection

It is advisable to reserve a table in advance at the more expensive restaurants, especially on Fridays, Saturdays and public holidays. Correct dress is appreciated everywhere and is essential in the top restaurants. Even in the simplest restaurants you should wait to be seated. A waiter or a special hostess will lead you to your table and hand you the menu, which in most establishments is written in Chinese and English.

Dried mushrooms
A practised fish cook

The selection below represents only a fraction of what is available in Hong Kong; for further information, visitors should consult the Hong Kong Tourist Association's *Dining and Entertainment* guide, available from HKTA Information and Gift Centres.

American Restaurant
20 Lockhart Road, Wanchai, tel: 2527 1000. Traditional restaurant serving Peking duck.

Blue Heaven
2/F, 48 Queen's Road, Central, tel: 2524 3001. Venerable *dim sum* restaurant with old ladies pushing the trollies; highly recommended for lunch.

Carrianna
2/F, Hilton Tower, 96 Granville Road, Tsim Sha Tsui East, tel: 2724 4828. Chiu Chow cuisine with good goose and chicken dishes.

City Chiu Chow
1/F, Allied Kajima Building, 138 Gloucester Road, Wanchai, tel: 2598 4333. Specialises in seafood; recommended are oyster omelette, deep-fried crab cakes and braised squid rolls.

Dynasty
Victoria Hotel, 200 Connaught Road, Western District, tel: 2540 7228, Ext. 7401. Opulent restaurant decorated in Tang Dynasty style, with a wide selection of Cantonese specialities.

Gaylord
1/F, Ashley Centre, 23-25 Ashley Road, Tsim Sha Tsui, tel: 2376 1001. North and South Indian cuisine with seafood and vegetarian dishes.

Hei Fung Terrace
1/F, The Repulse Bay, 109 Repulse Bay Road, Repulse Bay, tel: 2812 2622. Colourful mixture of Chinese cuisines in an elegant atmosphere in what used to be the Repulse Bay Hotel.

House of Canton
101 Caroline Centre, 2 Yun Ping Road, Causeway Bay, tel: 2882 1383. *Dim sum* at lunchtime, Cantonese specialities with a few Northern dishes at night.

Kublai's
151 Lockhart Road, Wanchai, tel: 2511 2287. Mongolian hot plate meal where guests fill their dishes at the buffet and have them cooked on hot plates in the kitchen.

Mughal Room
1/F, Carfield Commercial Building, 75-77 Wyndham Street, Central, tel: 2524 0107. Excellent Indian restaurant; not cheap, but serving outstanding Tandoori dishes.

Eat outdoors and enjoy the view

Nice Fragrance Vegetarian Kitchen
105–7 Thomson Road, Wanchai, tel: 2838 3067. A speciality cuisine based only on soya bean curd and vegetables. Pleasant, simple decor and friendly staff.

Peking Garden
Alexandra House, Charter Road, Central, tel: 2525 5688. Daily noodle-making performances; specialises in Northern cuisine

Red Pepper
7 Lan Fong Road, Causeway Bay, tel: 2577 3811. Spicy Szechuan dishes in all variations.

Hotel Nikko
72 Mody Road, Tsim Sha Tsui East, tel: 2739 1111. Even in Hong Kong, Japanese restaurants are expensive. This one, in a hotel, has a good selection of sushi and sashimi.

Shanghai Garden
Hutchison House, 10 Harcourt Road, Central, tel: 2524 8181. Shanghai cuisine with several good eel dishes, prawns and soya bean curd specialities.

Stanley's Oriental

Stanley's Oriental
90B, Stanley Main Street, Stanley, tel: 2813 9988. Pan-Asian cuisine of high quality in a renovated house on the seafront promenade at Stanley, in the south of Hong Kong.

Tin Tin Hot Pot
6/F, Island Centre, Causeway Bay, tel: 2890 9966. The Mongolian fire pot is especially popular in winter.

Yung Kee
32-40 Wellington Street, Central, tel: 2522 1624. Traditional restaurant specialising in goose and preserved eggs.

Nightlife

Sunset over the harbour

Nightclubs, bars and discos

The visitor has a wide choice of nightclubs, from Western-style dinner-dance restaurants and casual Chinese nightclubs, to plush cabaret restaurants with floor shows. Of course there are myriad girlie bars at which lonesome night owls can hire a succession of exotic table companions. Many of these are to be found in Wanchai, which to this day has failed to shake off its sexy 'Suzie Wong' image, although there are a number of quite ordinary restaurants and bars, particularly in Lockhart Road.

77

Many of the more expensive hostess clubs are to be found in a forest of flashing neon signs in Tsim Sha Tsui East. They feature elegant décor, excellent music and a wide choice of international hostesses for conversation and company.

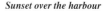

The younger set mostly heads for Lan Kwai Fong, two streets lined with bars and discos above the Central District. Tsim Sha Tsui also has quite a selection of bars and pubs, many of them in Ashley Road or the side streets off Carnarvon Road. If you want to play it safe, head for one of the bars and discotheques in the larger hotels, which tend to be packed on Friday, Saturday and the eves of public holidays, when premium charges apply. The action usually doesn't begin until around 10pm and continues well into the small hours. Hong Kong's top disco is 'JJ's' at the Grand Hyatt Hotel.

The Cactus Club
Night lights in Jordan Road

Food first

Before setting out to paint the town red, however, you should ensure your tanks are well filled. For the Chinese this means a generous dinner with as many companions as possible (*see page 73*). Many visitors will prefer to pick a restaurant for its view rather than its food. Some afford

Night view from The Peak

a spectacular view of the harbour, whilst others lie directly on a bay, for example around Repulse Bay or along Stanley Main Street. You could also take the ferry to the island of Lamma or Cheung Chau. Only minutes after selecting your supper from amongst the fish swimming in tanks in the seafood restaurants by the harbour it will reappear on your plate. On clear nights, take in the breathtaking panorama from The Peak, where there are two cafés that serve dinner. Since you may well not be the only person to think of this, it is a good idea to reserve a table. Harbour tours with meals included are also on offer, but for hygienic reasons it is advisable to steer clear of dinner on a sampan in one of the typhoon shelters.

Bright lights

For a constantly changing view of Hong Kong's bright lights, get on a tram in Central and travel to Causeway Bay. It is one of the cheapest nocturnal pleasures in town. Arriving at your destination you can spend some of the money you've saved in the shops.

Visitors can also head for the famous Night Market on Temple Street north of Kowloon Park, whose stalls only begin to open after 6pm. This can be followed by a leisurely stroll along the Kowloon promenade, the lights of Hong Kong island providing one of the most breathtaking nighttime panoramas in the world.

Horse racing

During the winter months, from September to May, there is horse racing twice a week in Happy Valley and Shatin. It's a worthwhile pastime even if you don't intend to risk a few dollars on a bet, but prefer to watch the experts and soak up the atmosphere on the vast stands.

Cinema

Hong Kong is also a film-makers' city. Its wide range of cinemas offer international films, mostly in English with Chinese subtitles.

Classical culture

With so many modern distractions, classical culture tends to take second place. Despite earnest efforts on the part of the government and other bodies, except for the festival weeks Hong Kong has never become a cultural mecca. Nonetheless, there are concerts by the Symphony Orchestra with guest peformances by visiting stars. Local repertory groups put on regular theatre productions either in English or Cantonese. The daily newspapers publish a calendar of events, brochures are available at City Hall and in the Arts Centre, and hotel concierges are a mine of local information.

Shopping and Markets

Indian tailors display their wares

With an almost endless array of goods available, Hong Kong continues to be a shopping paradise. It has long ceased to be a bargain, however. This is particularly so in the case of electronics where inflation and exorbitant rents have pared down the difference between local and European prices. Would-be purchasers should be wary of confidence tricksters who sell fake goods in original packages. It is essential to check prices at home, and to obtain an international guarantee. Highly recommended are member outlets of the Hong Kong Tourist Association (HKTA); they can be recognised by the sign on the door, a black junk on an red background. A list of these outlets is contained in the HKTA's free *Shopping Guide*.

79

The clothing on offer in the city's countless designer boutiques is also not much cheaper than in Europe or the United States, although there is a wide range of cheap merchandise available in the shops and markets, e.g. in Temple Street and in Stanley. Made-to-measure clothing is good value, provided the tailor has sufficient time to do a good job. Two fittings are necessary for a suit if it is to fit properly. Watches and jewellery are available in vast profusion. Here, too, a receipt is essential. The price of gold varies according to the current market value, and the amount of gold in an item of jewellery must be precisely stated. Jade is a green or white precious stone much loved by the Chinese. When choosing jade, make sure that the stone has a translucent lustre to it: avoid stones that have a milky appearance. If you plan to invest large sums, it is advisable to take along an expert.

Watches galore

The same applies to antiques, which are offered for sale mainly in Hollywood Road above the Central district. Prices are high and there are many fakes, some of them sold with certificates of authenticity.

Hollywood Road antique store

Depending on their origins, Hong Kong's department stores stock a varying range of goods. The chains based in the People's Republic offer goods produced there: porcelain, foodstuffs and souvenirs as well as silk and furniture. These days, international manufacturers produce many items, including clothing, shoes, toys and suitcases, in China and you will find brands meant for export selling in Hong Kong. Japanese department stores tend to cater to the luxury market shoppers and offer goods from all over the world in boutique-style departments. Lane Crawford, originally a British department store, can look back on many years of colonial history. Today, it too is largely organised as a series of boutiques, although it still offers all the items required by the English middle classes.

Carpet sellers

Expensive home furnishings and accessories are sold at shops that import their goods from Europe's leading glass and porcelain manufacturers. Carpets from China, Tibet, Pakistan, Afghanistan and India are available in abundance. Expensive silverware and toys such as fountain pens and lighters make attractive presents. Inexpensive sports equipment is also widely available.

80

Souvenir mask

Although department stores have fixed prices, bargaining is an almost essential part of the game. You can usually expect a better deal if you pay cash instead of using a credit card. Do not expect huge discounts, however, as prices tend to be fairly rigid everywhere. It is better to compare prices in one district with another rather than between shops along the same street.

Shopping centres
Ocean Centre, Ocean Terminal, Harbour City, 3-27 Canton Road, Tsim Sha Tsui. Acres of boutiques and shops, mostly selling clothing and shoes.
The Landmark, 16 Des Voeux Road, Central. Exclusive boutiques in a building with a large atrium.
Pacific Place, 88 Queensway, Central. Light, bright new centre on the boundary between Central and Wanchai.

Chinese department stores
Chinese Arts and Crafts, Prince's Building, 3 Des Voeux Road, Central; Silvercord Centre, 30 Canton Road, Tsim Sha Tsui. A wide range of items produced in China and traditional products e.g. porcelain, silk and craft items.
Chinese Merchandise Emporium, 92–104 Queen's Road, Central; Tower 1, Argyle Centre, 65 Argyle Street, Mongkok. Less expensive Chinese chain.

Hong Kong department store
Lane Crawford, Crawford House, 70 Queen's Road, Central; further shops in Pacific Place and Ocean Terminal. Long-established store with a wide range of goods.

Jewellery display

Japanese department stores

Mitsukoshi, 500 Hennessy Road, Causeway Bay; Sun Plaza, 28 Canton Road, Tsim Sha Tsui. An exclusive selection of goods presented in a series of boutiques; lovely Japanese porcelain.

Seibu, Pacific Place, 88 Queensway, Central. The best of the best, from antique furniture to French artichokes.

Sogo, 555 Hennessy Road, Causeway Bay. An entire floor of perfumes, several floors of women's and men's clothing plus a wide range of sports items.

Tailors

Bel Homme, 804 Mansion House, 74–8 Nathan Road, Tsim Sha Tsui.

Pacific Custom Tailors, 322 Pacific Place, 88 Queensway, Central.

Shirts 'N Shirts, 1001 Cheong Hing Building, 72 Nathan Road, Tsim Sha Tsui.

Y. William Yu, 46 Mody Road, Tsim Sha Tsui.

Street stalls and lanes

Western District: the Hollywood Road/Lok Ku Road area offers everything from antique works of art, porcelain and furniture, to modern reproductions.

Tea ware

Central: Li Yuen Street East and Li Yuen Street West for inexpensive clothes, handbags, costume jewellery and household goods in a true bazaar atmosphere; Theatre Lane for shoeshine services and repairs, locksmiths and engravers; Pottinger Street for haberdashery, buttons and bows, brushes, combs and hair ornaments, etc.; Man Wa Lane for traditional Chinese chops (seals) in jade, bone and hard stone; Western Market for a wide range fabrics and handicrafts from all over the world.

Causeway Bay: Jardine's Crescent for garments, fashion accessories and household goods in a real street market, and Jardine's Bazaar for dried foods, bean curd (tofu) and other traditional products.

Kowloon: the Ladies Market in Tung Choi Street in Mong Kok offers inexpensive local ladies' fashions and accessories; the Jade Market in Kansu Street, opposite Yau Ma Tei fruit market, is open daily from 10am to 3.30pm; the Temple Street Night Market sells sweaters, shirts, gadgets, CDs and much more, and is best visited after 8pm.

Factory outlets

Located in all major shopping areas but mainly in Central District, Cameron Road in Tsim Sha Tsui and Hung Hom (Kowloon), these sell a wide range of export garments including some designer items. The HKTA publishes a list of recommended outlets, available free from their Information and Gift Centres.

Getting There

By air

Even after 1997, Cathay Pacific Airlines will remain Hong Kong's flag carrier. In addition, more than 30 European and other Asian airlines have flights to Hong Kong. Travel agents specialising in Far Eastern travel can often offer very attractive all-in arrangements covering air tickets and accommodation.

Security is very rigid at Hong Kong International Airport. Nearly all the airlines X-ray all baggage before it is checked in. All hand carry items are either X-rayed or manually inspected.

Hong Kong International Airport is approximately 20 minutes' drive by car from all major hotels in Kowloon and less than 40 minutes' drive via the Cross-Harbour Tunnel from all major hotels on Hong Kong Island (rush-hour excepted). The new airport known as Chek Lap Kok on Lantau island is scheduled for completion in 1997, at which point Kai Tak will close.

The air-conditioned Airbus service operates between Hong Kong International Airport and popular areas of the city; it also stops at most major hotels. The A1 goes to the Star Ferry in Kowloon, the A2 to the Macau Ferry Terminal in the Western District and the A3 to Causeway Bay. It is essential to acquire small change beforehand, as the fare must be paid on boarding the bus and no change is given. A recorded announcement lists the hotels in the vicinity of each bus stop.

Getting a taxi is not difficult, either. The queue which sometimes forms by the taxi rank quickly disappears.

Return and onward flights must be reconfirmed at least 36 hours before departure. Hotels will undertake this service for their guests. In order to ensure punctual take-off, all check-in counters close 40 minutes before, and gates 10 minutes before, the scheduled departure time. Punctuality is essential.

Hong Kong airport departure tax is HK$ 50 for adults (1995 rate). There is no charge for children under 13.

By sea

For those with plenty of time and very ample means, a half-dozen cruise lines include Hong Kong on their 'Exotic East' or 'Round the World' grand tours. Among the current vessels that tie up at Ocean Terminal (Hong Kong's well placed and serviced passenger wharf) are ships from the Norwegian America Line, Royal Viking Line, Holland America Line and, of course, P&O. Passenger-carrying freighters are slightly less expensive. American President Lines (San Francisco) and Glen and Shire Lines (London) make frequent Pacific runs.

The luxury way to go

Getting Around

Hong Kong has a remarkable range of public transport facilities which are both efficient and inexpensive. Some can even claim to be amongst the city's most famous sights.

The MTR is clean and efficient

The underground

The MTR (Mass Transit Railway) runs along three routes: the Tsuen-Wan Route from Central through the Harbour Tunnel to Kowloon and towards the Western New Territories as far as Tsuen Wan; the Kwung-Tong Route from Yau Ma Tei on the Kowloon Peninsula to Kowloon Bay and the Eastern Harbour Tunnel to Quarry Bay, where there is a connection to the Island Line; and finally the Island Line along the north coast of Hong Kong Island between Sheung Wan in the west and Chai Wan in the east.

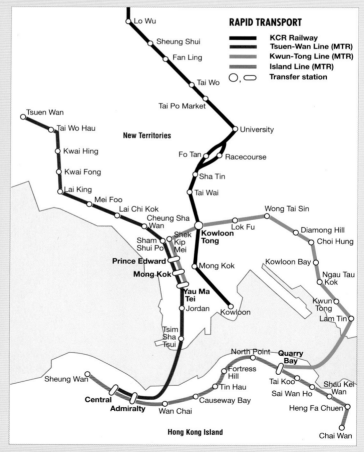

RAPID TRANSPORT

▬▬▬	KCR Railway
▬▬▬	Tsuen-Wan Line (MTR)
▬▬▬	Kwun-Tong Line (MTR)
▬▬▬	Island Line (MTR)
○, ▭	Transfer station

Lo Wu
Sheung Shui
Fan Ling
Tai Wo
Tai Po Market
University

Tsuen Wan
Tai Wo Hau
Kwai Hing
Kwai Fong
Lai King
Mei Foo
Lai Chi Kok
Cheung Sha Wan
Sham Shui Po
Shek Kip Mei
Prince Edward
Mong Kok
Yau Ma Tei
Jordan
Tsim Sha Tsui

New Territories

Fo Tan
Racecourse
Sha Tin
Tai Wai

Wong Tai Sin
Lok Fu
Kowloon Tong
Diamong Hill
Choi Hung
Mong Kok
Kowloon Bay
Ngau Tau Kok
Kowloon
Kwun Tong
Lam Tin

North Point
Quarry Bay
Fortress Hill
Tin Hau
Tai Koo
Shau Kei Wan
Sai Wan Ho
Heng Fa Chuen

Sheung Wan
Central
Admiralty
Wan Chai
Causeway Bay

Hong Kong Island

Chai Wan

The MTR is the fastest and most efficient means of transport, although, of course, it offers little by way of views. The cost depends on the route taken. Passengers purchase a plastic card which is encoded at the barrier. If you plan to use the underground frequently it would be worthwhile buying a multi-journey ticket (Common Stored Value Ticket), which is available for HK$70, $100 or $200 (1995 prices). Near the exits of MTR stations will be found a sketch map of the surroundings to help you find the correct exit. At most stations you will also find shops and a bank counter.

Kowloon-Canton Railway (KCR)

This suburban-type railway departs from Hung Hom station in Kowloon and runs as far as the border station at Lowu. The intermediate stations provide convenient access to the towns and villages of the New Territories; the farthest you can go go without a China visa is Sheung Shui. The MTR multi-journey tickets are valid, and there is an interchange between the two systems at Kowloon Tong station. Trains run thoughout the day.

Light Rail Transit (LRT)

The LRT serves the New Territories

This is a high-speed surface system linking the New Territories Towns of Tuen Mun and Yuen Long. The LRT runs from 5.30am to 12.30 am on weekdays and from 6am to midnight on Sunday and public holidays. Fares start at HK$3 (1995 prices).

Tram

The tram is the ideal means of transport for short trips along the north coast of Hong Kong Island or for a leisurely outing, especially at night, through the streets of Wanchai and Causeway Bay. The entrance is at the rear, and you should give yourself ample time to get to the exit at the front, where adults toss HK$ 1.20 and children 60 cents into the fare box on disembarking (1995 prices).

Peak Tram

For more than a century the Peak Tram has provided the quickest way of ascending The Peak. The tram takes only 7–8 minutes to cover the 0.9-mile/1.4-km route whilst ascending to 1,174ft (367m). The best views can be obtained from a window seat on the right-hand side of the car. The tram runs approximately every 15 minutes until midnight. Prices in 1995: Adults HK$10 (single), HK$16 (return); children HK$4 (single), HK$6 (return).

Buses

Double-decker buses, which run from 6am till midnight, cover most parts of the territory. The fare is not dependent

Buses are cheap

upon the length of journey, but solely on the point of entry. A table near the driver gives the necessary information. The fare is put into a box (no change) upon entry. Route numbers are difficult to decipher, but the HKTA has a leaflet for visitors listing the main routes.

Minibuses

Yellow with a red stripe, these cover fixed routes, although they stop anywhere to pick up passengers, who indicate that they wish to embark by holding out their arm. To disembark, one simply shouts. The fare is listed on a table, or the driver simply announces the cost when one disembarks. Fares range from HK$2 to HK$7 (1995 prices).

Maxicabs

Yellow with a green stripe, these run along specific routes and have fixed prices ranging from HK$1 to HK$8. A sign on the front indicates the destination. Pay as you get in.

Ferries

No trip to Hong Kong is complete without a trip across the harbour on the Star Ferry. In operation since 1898, it links the tip of Tsim Sha Tsui with Central District and covers a second route to Wanchai. At HK$1.50 (upper deck) and HK$1.20 (lower deck), it must be one of the cheapest and most scenic ferry rides in the world. Fares are paid at the automatic turnstiles at the entrance. The service runs from 6.30am to 11.30pm and the crossing takes approximately eight minutes.

Ferries run approximately every hour between the Outlying Districts Pier and the islands of Lantau, Lamma, Peng Chau and Cheung Chau. Most islands can be reached more rapidly by hoverferry, although the latter only runs three or four times a day. A fast ferry also runs from the Star Ferry Pier to Discovery Bay on Lantau. Also from the Outlying Districts Pier is a hovercraft link with Tuen Mun in the Western New Territories; there are also further connections to Jordan and Hung Hom.

Taxi

Inner city cabs

Hong Kong taxis have signs on the roof and a red plate proclaiming 'For Hire' on the windscreen. In the inner city they are red with silver roofs, in the New Territories, green with white roofs and on Lantau they are blue with white roofs. The driver must switch on the meter at the start of the journey. There is a basic charge for red taxis for the first 1¼ miles (2km), then an extra charge for every 200m. The other taxis are somewhat cheaper. Double tunnel fees (HK$20 in 1995) are charged for crossing the harbour; large items of luggage cost around HK$ 5. Check rates at the time of your visit.

Facts for the Visitor

Discussing itineraries

Visas

Most visitors need only a valid passport for entry. UK citizens are allowed 6 months; Western European and Commonwealth passport holders 3 months; US and Canadian citizens one month. There are no changes to be made to these requirements post 1997.

Customs

Hong Kong is a free port and taxes are only levied on alcohol, tobacco and perfume. The tax-free allowances are one litre wine or spirits, 200 cigarettes or 250g tobacco, 60ml perfume or 250ml eau de toilette. There are no restrictions on exports, but regulations of the country of destination should be borne in mind. Hong Kong remains a free port after 1997 and the allowances will not change.

Tourist information

The Hong Kong Tourist Association (HKTA) is the official government-sponsored body representing the entire tourism industry in Hong Kong.

In the UK: 4th/5th Floors, 125 Pall Mall, London SW1Y 5EA, tel: 0171-930 4755.

In the US: 5th Floor, 590 Fifth Avenue, New York, NY 10036-4706, tel: 212-869 5008/9; Suite 1220, 10940 Wilshire Boulevard, Los Angeles, CA 90024-3915, tel: 310-208 4582; Suite 200, 610 Enterprise Drive, Oak Brook, IL 60521, tel: 708-575 2828.

In Hong Kong: 35th Floor, Jardine House, 1 Connaught Place, Central, Hong Kong, tel: 852-2801 7111; Information Service (multilingual), tel: 2807 6177.

HKTA Information and Gift Centres: International Airport (Buffer Hall, daily 8am–10.30pm); Star Ferry Con-

See Hong Kong from the water

course Kowloon (Monday to Friday 8am–6pm, Saturday, Sunday and public holidays 9am–5pm); Shop 8, Basement, Jardine House, 1 Connaught Place, Central (Monday to Friday 8am–6pm, Saturday 9am–1pm, closed Sunday and public holidays).

Sightseeing tours

The HKTA organises special tours and programmes on a regular basis. These include 'The Land Between' Tour, Sports and Recreation Tour, Come Horseracing Tour, Heritage Tours and Family Insight Tour. Brochures are available at the information and gift centres.

Star Ferry and Watertours arrange excursions and harbour sightseeing trips including lunch or dinner. Reservations can be made through hotels or at the Star Ferry Pier, tel: 2366 7024, Watertours, tel: 2525 4808.

Junks and other boats can be chartered from Simpson Marine, tel: 2555 8377

To rent out a sailing boat it is necessary to be a member of one of the sailing clubs.

Currency and exchange

There is no limit on the import or export of foreign currency. The local currency is the Hong Kong Dollar (HK$) which is pegged loosely to the US Dollar at an approximate rate of US$1 to HK$7.80, although the rate does vary slightly. Banknotes are issued by three different banks and have different motifs but similar colours. Banknotes are available in the following denominations: HK$ 1,000, 500, 100, 50, 20 and 10. Coins are available to the value of HK$ 5, 2 and 1 as well as 50, 20 and 10 cents.

All valid credit cards are accepted without query in the larger hotels, restaurants and shops. There are large numbers of cash dispensers. American Express cardholders have access to Jetco automatic teller machines (ATMs) and can withdraw local currency and cash traveller's cheques at Express Cash ATMs. Holders of Visa and MasterCard can also obtain local currency from the Hongkong Bank ATMs at convenient locations.

Banks, licensed money changers and hotels will exchange cash and encash traveller's cheques. Banks charge commission up to HK$30 for cash exchanges, and HK$50 for traveller's cheques. Hotels and money changers charge no commission but offer less favourable exchange rates. Traveller's cheques can be encashed free of charge by the issuing company:

American Express, New World Tower, 16–18 Queen's Road Central; Thomas Cook, 18/F, Vicwood Plaza, 199 Des Voeux Road Central.

Major banks are open Monday to Friday 9am–4.30pm or 5pm, Saturday 9am–12.30pm or 1pm.

Tipping
Tipping is always welcomed. Most restaurants add a 10 percent service charge to the bill; if the service is particularly good, guests should leave a few coins or – in the case of larger bills, a few notes – on the table, adding up to approximately another 10 percent.

The hotel porters who carry your luggage usually expect to receive about HK$10–20, and in top hotels even more. The friendly attendants in the washrooms who turn on the taps and pass you the towels normally receive HK$1–2.

Local people seldom tip taxi drivers, but, like taxi drivers all over the world, they will be very glad if you do give them something extra.

Souvenirs
Hong Kong is a shopping paradise in which there is almost nothing money cannot buy. This means that there are also items here which travellers should refrain from purchasing. According to the Washington Accord on Protected Species, the import and export of endangered animals, and products derived from such creatures, are strictly forbidden. In Hong Kong, this applies in particular to ivory. Products derived from tigers and rhinoceroses are revered in Chinese mysticism for their aphrodisiac properties, but these too are banned.

Shop opening times
There are no legal restrictions; the following times may be taken as a guide:
Tsim Sha Tsui, Yaumatei, Mongkok: 10am–9pm
Tsim Sha Tsui East: 10am–7.30pm
Central: 10am–6pm; Sunday: many shops closed
Wanchai, Causeway Bay: 10am–9.30pm

Postal services
The main post offices are on Hong Kong Island, next to the Star Ferry (Monday to Friday 8am–6pm; Saturday 8am–2pm) and in Kowloon between Jordan and Yau Ma Tei MTR stations (Monday to Friday 9.30am–6pm; Saturday 9.30am–1pm). There are numerous branch post offices throughout the city, which have shorter opening hours. All post offices close on Sunday and public holidays. Hotels usually sell postage stamps and will mail guests' post if requested.

Familiar post box

Telephone
In principle, local calls in Hong Kong are free of charge. Nonetheless, hotels charge HK$3–5, and in the case of telephone booths or the big yellow phones the user must insert HK$1. Long-distance calls are cheaper than in Eu-

Keeping up communications

rope (HK$12.50 per minute to Western Europe). They can be made from International Direct Dialling (IDD) Public Coin Phones, and by Cardphone, as well as from offices of H.K. Telecom International Ltd; the following offices are open 24 hours a day, including public holidays: 102A, One Exchange Square, Central; Hermes House, 10 Middle Road, Tsim Sha Tsui.

Call 013 for information on dial access numbers and details on phone locations, purchase and operation of stored-value phone cards (HK$50, $100, $150 and $200) and coin phones. Stored-value phone cards (HK$50) can also be purchased at HKTA Information and Gift Centres. Most hotels have IDD and some charge a handling fee. All charges given here are 1995 rates.

International dialling codes: to Hong Kong: 852 (no additional code is required for subscribers within the city limits); from Hong Kong, dial 001 (telephone) or 002 (fax), followed by the country code, the exchange code (without the zero) and finally the subscriber's number.

Time
Hong Kong time is GMT plus 8 hours. In summer Hong Kong is only 7 hours ahead of the United Kingdom as there is no Summer Time.

Voltage
The voltage is 220V/50Hz almost everywhere. However, three-pin plugs of various sizes and shapes are required to fit the sockets. Adaptors are available in hotels and supermarkets, and at better hotels you will find sockets for electric shavers and built-in hair driers.

Units of measurement
There is a great deal of confusion about this. For a number of years now attempts have been made to introduce the metric system, with only partial success. At the same time you will find English pounds and ounces. Beer is usually measured in pints, but sometimes in decilitres. Metres and kilometres have established themselves as the official measure of distance, but area is still calculated in square feet.

To complicate matters still further, market stallholders and fishmongers prefer to weigh their wares in Chinese *catty*, for which they use a spring balance.

Handicapped visitors
With its steep paths, narrow stairways and the priority given to cars everywhere, Hong Kong is not an easy city for the handicpaped. Recently, some efforts have been made to improve the situation. The HKTA has prepared a brochure for the disabled with helpful tips.

Public holidays

The most important Western, Christian, Chinese and religious festivals are all observed. Most shops remain open for at least half a day on these special days, except during Chinese New Year. Traditional Chinese festivals are based on the lunar calendar and therefore vary from year to year.

1 January	New Year's Day
January/February	Chinese New Year (three days)
April	Good Friday, Easter
April	Festival of the Dead (Ching Ming)
End of August	Bank Holiday
September	Moon Festival
October	Mountain Festival (Chung Yeung)
25–7 December	Christmas

Television

There are two English-language channels. Programmes include a selection of locally produced shows as well as features from the UK, the United States and Australia. Also available is STAR TV (a satellite channel) and, in some areas, Cable TV.

Radio

Six English-language channels provide a wide range of programmes. The BBC World Service is also relayed from 4am to 12.15am.

Newspapers

The two most respected English-language newspapers are the *South China Morning Post* and the *Eastern Express*; the *Hong Kong Standard* is inferior as regards both reputation and quality. Apart from daily news, you will also find information about events, cinema programmes and on Wednesday (during the racing season) a supplement devoted to horse racing. *HK*, a newspaper covering bars, restaurants and gossip, is distributed free of charge.

Photography

Apart from camps and military complexes there are no restrictions on photography. Nonetheless, photographers should bear in mind the rights of the individual to his or her privacy. The rickshaw drivers by the Star Ferry Pier on Central and the Hakka women in the New Territories will only pose for a fee of approximately HK$20–30.

Films and developing studios will be found on every street corner.

Dress

Loose-fitting light clothing made of natural fibres is suitable almost all the year round. Revealing attire and casual sports gear are not appreciated by the local residents except in the appropriate places. For all business encounters, exercise prudence and dress conservatively. The same applies in many restaurants at night.

Health precautions

No vaccinations are required to enter Hong Kong. During the past few years there have been a number of cases of hepatitis and food poisoning, caused by insufficiently cooked fish and seafood from the heavily polluted Hong Kong coastal waters or by green leafy vegetables from China which had been contaminated by pesticides. It is advisable to exercise caution when eating from street stalls. There have been no reported cases of illness from food consumed in the larger restaurants or hotels.

The excessively cool temperatures in air-conditioned buildings may lead to a chill when the weather is hot and humid outside. A jacket or pullover affords protection. A sunhat and suntan lotion are necessary for extended periods outdoors.

Medical

Most hospitals offer services to a high medical standard. The doctors are trained in Western or Chinese medicine and usually speak English as they have studied abroad. Treatment must be paid for in cash; check with your health insurance company beforehand concerning the procedure for claiming reimbursement. Medicines are widely available. Doctors often sell the necessary medicines in their clinics; chemist's shops are also well stocked. For the sake of convenience, travellers should bring adequate supplies of commonly used medicines. Hotels will assist if you need a doctor in an emergency. For ambulance service in Kowloon, tel: 2713 5555; on Hong Kong Island, tel: 2576 6555.

Emergencies

Police, Fire, Ambulance, tel: 999

Lost and found

There is no official lost property office. Enquiries must be made in the vicinity where the loss occurred or at the transport offices in question. It is better to offer a member of staff at the hotel a generous tip in return for assistance, as without a knowledge of Cantonese, your search is bound to be fruitless.

Diplomatic representation

British Consulate, c/o HK Immigration, Wanchai Tower II, 7 Gloucester Road, Hong Kong, tel: 2824 6111.
Consulate of the United States of America, 26 Garden Road, Central, Hong Kong, tel: 2523 9011.

Accommodation

The lobby of the Grand Hyatt

Hong Kong has more than a hundred hotels of international standard, and virtually all the larger groups and chains have at least one establishment here. However, since the city is such a popular destination for business and pleasure travellers, rooms are almost always fully booked despite the large number of beds available.

It is therefore highly recommended that you reserve accommodation before departure through a travel agent specialising in Asia. The best prices are often obtained through an air ticket and accommodation package.

Hong Kong's hotels are proud of their standards of quality and service. Most also offer good sports facilities, bars and restaurants. Hotel restaurants play a more important role on the gourmet stage here than they do in Europe and the US. It is common for local residents to invite their guests to dinner at hotel restaurants or meet after business in the bars.

Location is often a good criterion in deciding where to stay. Many tourists prefer the hotels in Tsim Sha Tsui, the tip of Kowloon, an area which is always very lively. An alternative is Tsim Sha Tsui East, where the prices are somewhat higher and public transport connections less favourable. The hotels further up Nathan Road, in Yaumatei and Mongkok, are cheaper. The most expensive hotels are in Central, where you will also find the Central Plaza shopping centre and the Conference Centre. In the old part of Wanchai can be found smaller, inexpensive hotels. Causeway Bay, which enjoys good public transport facilities, is the favoured location of a number of hotels preferred by tour groups.

Tucked away in the New Territories is a hotel which claims to be Hong Kong's first resort complex. It is also possible to stay overnight in Shatin. On the island of Lan-

tau or the smaller Cheung Chau you can even escape the madding crowd.

There are not really any viable alternatives to the hotels. The Pensions which let rooms to visitors are not to be recommended, on the whole. For members, however, there are seven youth hostels in Hong Kong, some of which are very attractive indeed.

Hotel selection

Century, 238 Jaffe Road, Wanchai, tel: 2598 8888; fax: 2598 8866. Not luxurious, but in the heart of Wanchai.

Excelsior, 281 Gloucester Road, Causeway Bay, tel: 2894 8888; fax: 2895 6459. Well-run, compact hotel with good access to public transport.

Furama Kempinski, 1 Connaught Road, Central, tel: 2848 7444; fax: 2801 4738. Hotel in the upper price category. Convenient location in Central.

Holiday Inn Golden Mile, 50 Nathan Road, Tsim Sha Tsui, tel: 2369 3111; fax: 2369 8016. Popular hotel along Kowloon's shopping thoroughfare, with a German restaurant and delicatessen.

Hyatt Regency, 67 Nathan Road, Tsim Sha Tsui, tel: 2311 1234; fax: 2739 8701. Upper-category hotel along the Nathan Road shopping thoroughfare.

Island Shangri-La, 88 Queensway, Central, tel: 2877 3838; fax: 2521 8742. The flagship of the Shangri-La group with elegant furnishings and pleasant service. Above the Pacific Place shopping complex.

The Park Lane, 310 Gloucester Road, Causeway Bay, tel: 2890 3355; fax: 2890 3620. Relaxing view across Victoria Park in this attractive, well-run hotel. Good transport facilities.

The Peninsula, Salisbury Road, Tsim Sha Tsui, tel: 2366 6251; fax: 2722 4170. This epitome of colonial hotels has given in to high-tech creature comforts with its new tower extension. The lobby still boasts golden chandeliers.

The Royal Pacific, 33 Canton Road, Tsim Sha Tsui, tel: 2738 2222; fax: 2736 5119. Excellent value for money above the shopping paradise of Ocean Centre.

Hotel Victoria, 200 Connaught Road, Western District, tel: 2540 7228; fax: 2517 1577. Efficient hotel by the Macau ferry pier, near the famous Western District.

Index